DOING TIME

By
Guy Opperman MP

Prisons in the 21st Century

First Published 2012
Copyright © Guy Opperman 2012

Guy Opperman asserts his moral rights to be considered to be the author of this work.

Bretwalda Books
Unit 8, Fir Tree Close, Epsom, Surrey KT17 3LD
www.BretwaldaBooks.com

ISBN 978-1-909099-03-6

Bretwalda Books Ltd

About the Author

Guy Opperman was elected the Conservative MP for Hexham in May 2010. He had a varied career as a jockey, criminal barrister and businessman before his election to the House of Commons. He gave his maiden speech on the subject of prison reform and changes to the criminal justice system.

Guy spent 20 years as a barrister – 15 years of which were spent predominantly at the criminal bar. Guy prosecuted and defended in multiple murder and rape trials, and conducted hundreds of Crown Court trials all cross the country.

He was one of the key members of a local Free Representation Unit, which over a 7 year period provided free legal assistance in hundreds of cases on behalf of Victim Support and Citizens Advice Bureau. The scheme is now being copied nationwide. In 2007 Guy was awarded the Bar Pro Bono Award by the former Attorney General, Lord Goldsmith QC, both for his voluntary work on behalf of victims in Criminal Injuries Compensation Appeals, but also for his campaign against hospital closures in the town where he was born.

He has 20 years' experience of visiting prisons from Bristol and Durham, to Brixton and beyond, as a lawyer and MP. In 2009 the Attorney General, Baroness Scotland QC, gave him a Pro Bono Hero award in the House of Commons for his pro bono work campaigning to prevent hospital closures.

On weekends off he still rides as a slightly fat jockey.

Foreword

This book has taken over a year and a half to write, both because I was taken very ill in April 2011, and also because my real job is very much full time. The writing has been sandwiched into weekends and late night sittings, to the detriment of time spent with loved ones and family.

It could not have been written without the support, effort and encouragement of so many people to whom I am extremely grateful. Many of the former and serving prisoners or prison officers who have helped me have had to remain anonymous, but they all know who they are.

I owe a debt to a variety of House of Commons staff from the incredible House of Commons Library, to my work experience team this last year of Max Kuhnke and Kareem Elsawi. My professional staff have given up their evenings, weekends and holidays to assist with research, writing, redrafts and fact checking, as well as helping me on the long road back to fitness after I got ill in April 2011. I am eternally grateful therefore to the efforts of Jon Aydon, Peter McManus, and Charlie Campbell.

Various colleagues and professional organisations interested in prison reform, not least A4E and the Shannon Trust have assisted and read early drafts. The present Prisons Minister, Crispin Blunt, MP, who is both a good Prisons Minister and a colleague of mine, kindly sat down and read an early draft and came back with some comments and observations. This book is not a criticism of him or the present government.

Several family members and friends too numerous to name also assisted by reading early drafts and sub editing. My father was his usual robust self, and my stepmother, Abby Opperman, and my friend Karen Barichievy, both proof read working drafts at various stages.

No book gets written without a publisher, and the team at Bretwalda Books, notably Rupert Matthews and Adrian Thompson, have been very supportive and full of enthusiasm for the project.

I have not been paid in any way for producing this book, which is a labour of love to try to influence, and bring reform and improvement to the Prison Service that I believe in passionately. All royalties, after production and publishing expenses, will go to the neurological charity, the National Brain Appeal, which supports the hospital that saved my life.

This book is as accurate as it is possible to be as of late June 2012. However, all mistakes are most definitely mine.

Contents

Introduction

"Insanity: doing the same thing over and over again and expecting different results."
Albert Einstein

Prison does work. It locks people up so that the prisoner cannot then commit a crime: yet prison for years has failed to change the prisoner's behaviour. Despite multiple new laws, and successive politicians passing tougher and tougher sentences, the prisoners throughout the 1990s and throughout the Blair / Brown government still reoffended upon release in their tens of thousands. It is a disappointing fact of our prison system that under the last government released prisoners had a reoffending rate of approximately 70%. Previously, prisons were a short term fix, rather than a long term solution. Slowly this is beginning to change but prisons are not working as they could and should do.

The statistics on prison numbers and reoffending are overwhelming.

Prison Numbers:[1]	Total Number of Prisoners
• 1946:	14,556
• 1993:	42,991
• 2011:	85,951
• 16 March 2012:	87,870.

This figure has come down slightly since March 2012 but the harsh reality is that prisoners have more than doubled in the past 20 years.

For too long successive politicians have focused on the importance of deprivation of liberty – clinging to the notion that simple incarceration will change the criminal's ways. But the problem is more complex than that. If incarceration was effective, why do people keep reoffending, and why are our prisons getting fuller and fuller?

The public does not want us to be soft on prisoners. The Justice system needs to command the respect and confidence of the people. It clearly has not commanded that respect for some considerable time. Nor does it command the respect of the police force, 46% of whom, when polled, felt that prison was "not working". The police felt that prison did work in keeping criminals away from the public, even if only for a short amount of time, but that "prisoners were not spending their time in prison productively". Polling also showed that the failures of prison were due fundamentally to the prison itself not focusing enough on rehabilitating prisoners. Repeated polling shows that the public wants prison to be more effective at changing prisoners' behaviour. Put simply, it wants government to knuckle down and make prisons work[2].

This study attempts to analyse what went wrong with the prison regimes in the past, makes suggestions for future changes, and assesses how things are changing under the new government.

It is an attempt to:
Address the holy trinity of prison problems that is holding back progress – 50% drug use, 50% illiteracy and a failure to get prisoners working
• Identify what kind of prison system we would like to have
• Explore the potential for a charity or church / community based organisation to run a prison

• Address the payment-by-results programme that is being used to change the way privately run prisons are run
• Finally, this study will attempt to address the silo problems of the criminal justice system, and the way in which we deal with serious prisoners

Time in custody

There is a fundamental need to change what a prisoner does when in a prison. Prisoners are captive – we need to make the prison work to change the prisoner:

Large numbers of prisoners cannot read, write or do maths. There should be, where possible, a compulsory requirement for a prisoner to learn.

Prisoners should be required to learn a skill and do proper work both to repay victims and get them ready for release. Prisoners who do not take part in any education or training during their sentence are far more likely to reoffend once released[3].

Drugs are a constant scourge in prison: progress in rehabilitation will fail if we continue to have 50% of the prison under the influence of illegal or prescribed drugs.

Reoffending is the real problem that successive governments have failed to address. Compare the years 2000-2010: in 2010, more than 96,700 prisoners sentenced for serious crimes had at least 15 convictions or cautions. This is a drastic increase compared to the figure in 2000 of 54,200[4]. Over the past decade the number of prisoners recalled to prison has more than quadrupled to 100,000[5].

A change of Culture and Attitude

By ignoring prisoners, locking them up, and then discharging them with no basic skills, and still drug addicted, we have created a recipe for disaster and ever increasing prison numbers. This has produced a cycle of crime at great cost to the taxpayer. Steps are being taken and the coalition has clearly made a starter on a long journey of reform. But whilst the longest journey starts with the shortest step we will need to see this through. A liberal conservative government should make the tackling of crime and reoffending a number one priority. The key point is that we know what the problems are: all are capable of being addressed.

Guy Opperman
MP For Hexham
1st July 2012

Chapter 1:

Who goes to Prison?

As the Hexham MP I write as someone who has the old Hexham Gaol still standing to this day in the centre of the town of Hexham. Built in the 1330's it held prisoners captured in the Hexhamshire and the Border Marches. It is the oldest purpose built prison in England. It is now a museum[6].

Similarly the first Roman Prison has been unearthed at the Vindolanda fort, 13 miles west of Hexham, which is again in my constituency. Evidence suggests that Vindolanda Fort could have held many hundreds of prisoners just south of Hadrian's Wall in the third century. It appears to be the first ever prisoner of war camp[7].

As a criminal barrister I spent a lot of time in prisons. As an MP my interest is both as a constituency MP and as someone passionate about reform of these ancient institutions.

But very few members of the public actually go to prisons. Aside from families of prisoners, and the various support teams working inside, 4 types of people spend their time in prisons:
• Prisoners
• Prison Officers
• Governors
• And occasionally Politicians

Prisoners
Not everyone who goes to prison is a mass murderer, psychopath or child molester. But some are and they are

rightly incarcerated to ensure the protection of the public. I hope that the following chapters will show how the prison population is not what you might think it would be if you were a normal member of the public or tabloid reader.

It is clear that the majority of the prison population struggles to cope with the normal aspects of society that most people take for granted. This is not an excuse but to get an overview you cannot forget the statistical context. Bear in mind that:

• 25% of prisoners were in care as children – as compared to 2% for the rest of the population.

• Approximately half of all prisoners ran away from home as a child.

• 50% of male prisoners have been excluded from school;

• 33% of women prisoners have been excluded.

• 50% of male prisoners have no qualifications at all.

• 70% of female prisoners have no qualifications at all.

• 82% of prisoners have the writing ability of, or less than an 11 year old child.

Over a third has no permanent accommodation or had been sleeping rough before they entered prison.

Of all prisoners 43% have a family member who has been convicted of a criminal offence.

The Social Exclusion Unit and the House of Commons Library is full of such statistics. I have given a mere snapshot of what is sobering reading.

Understanding this background hopefully allows the education of the public to a more rational debate. No one is saying these people are blameless. But the causes of their decline from acceptable standards of moral society are there for all to see. It may be wrong to argue that such prisoners would inevitably commit crime but it is not hard to see why they fell by the wayside.

Other prisoners are often a little harder to assess:

What would you make of the following prisoners?
A fraudster?

A young man who stole the credit card of a close family friend and then spent large amounts of money defrauding lawful businesses with the card that was not his?

Dangerous no, but this was repeated offending that merited prison: He did several months for obtaining property by deception as a young man.

What of this terrorist?

A young man, arrested 2 miles outside the small village of Howick, on a dusty deserted road on the 5'thAugust 1962. That man was subsequently convicted of sabotage and other serious charges. He was sentenced to 27 years in prison.

It is of interest that in a recent poll of the two people that men and women in Britain would most like to have dinner with, both these two people came pretty close to the top.

The fraudster was Stephen Fry, who spent time in Pucklechurch Prison before becoming a celebrated author, humourist, TV Star and actor.

The second, of course, was Nelson Mandela. I have been to where Mandela was arrested as he tried to leave the Pietermaritzburg home of former African National Congress president Chief Albert Luthuli, after discussing the armed struggle against white South Africa.

Other former Prisoners

Or, what of Martin Luther King and Mahatma Gandhi? Both were inspirational and moving leaders who defined their countries. Both were prisoners. King's non-violent strategy was adopted by black students all over the South of the United States in protest against segregated transport, restaurant and lunch-counter segregation and segregation in public parks, swimming pools, theatres, churches, libraries, museums and beaches.

Eventually, in the campaign to end segregation at lunch counters in Birmingham Alabama, in the spring of 1963 King and large numbers of his supporters, including schoolchildren, were arrested and jailed. Whilst in Birmingham City Jail, on April 16th 1963, King wrote the famous open Letter from Birmingham Jail, in response to the statement made by eight white Alabama clergymen.

The list of those with unexpected past lives is endless and diverse – consider a melting pot that includes Keith Richards, Sophia Loren, Robert Downey Junior and Gandhi. The point is that all prisoners are different and have different reasons for being there. Not all are as eloquent, optimistic or right in the long run as Mahatma Gandhi:

"I care so deeply about this matter that I'm willing to take on the legal penalties, to sit in this prison cell, to sacrifice my freedom, in order to show you how deeply I care. Because when you see the depth of my concern, and how civil I am in going about this, you're bound to change your mind about me, to abandon your rigid, unjust position, and to let me help you see the truth of my cause."

Prison Officers:
On any interpretation Prison Officers do a very difficult job. It is worth remembering that our officers are

unarmed. Every prisoner and lawyer will have met good ones and bad ones. This is something that applies in every job. But it is also correct to say that you will not get significant change in the prison service without prison officers embracing their role in changing prisoner's behaviour. Officers need to understand that they are an integral part of the system and key component in change, and not the enemy.

There have been times when the service was not rowing in the same direction as its own Governors or the Service as a wider whole. Take the view of the former Director of Prisons, Derek Lewis, who in the 1990's described how the Prison Officers Association was a malevolent force, with a "*stubborn defence of restrictive practices, coupled with belligerent and threatening behaviour.*" This created, according to Lewis, an image of the service that was "*rooted in the past*". This has changed. But more needs to be done.

It is fair to say that the officers are given the most basic of training, but slowly this is being improved. One former prisoner argued strongly that officers,

"*Should be motivated by a need to understand and work with offenders, rather than just failed prison officers, who have no desire to know why someone ended up in prison.*"

There are significant aspects of mentoring which could be acquired through training that would make a difference.

This would involve:
• the officers learning how to become mentors to the prisoners;
• a mentorship programme for the officers themselves to share and learn best practice: continuous

improvement and accountability are some of the consequences of having a functioning mentorship scheme

However, the most important change will be a change to the officer's state of mind: if a prison officer regards him or herself as simply a prison security guard then real change in prisoner's behaviour will not occur. All sides in this complex structure will have to adapt and change if the longed for change in outcomes is to occur. On this issue it is worth making the point that the best prison officers are more often seen in the publicly provided prison service. In any organisation where cost targets are the only motivation to management then quality does not matter as much, leading to examples of lesser staff being used in some of the private prisons. Therefore, the way in which prison officers are incentivised needs to be addressed. A payment structure could be devised that provides a proper wage to prison officers but which also rewards those prison officers and governors in prisons which reduce offending and improve literacy, skills and drug treatment programmes. Just as you have payment-by-results in the new prisons so it should be in the prison service itself – with a dual cost and outcomes focus. Motivation by performance and enhanced pay through better outcomes has worked in a multitude of other sectors to the benefit of all. It can and would make a difference in a prison. Potentially it would also mean both more money, but more importantly, greater job satisfaction, for those who do this difficult and demanding job. The last word should go to one anonymous but highly motivated and interested observer, with great experience of the prison service, who confided to me:

"Poor quality and disinterested officers are the major

stumbling block to enabling rehabilitation in prisons. There needs to be a sea change in this area otherwise, no amount of good intention and effort by government and others will be stymied by the "black knights" of the system."

The Governor

"The most anxious man in a prison is the governor."
George Bernard Shaw

Multiple films have by and large given the Governor a bad reputation. Most of the time, this is manifestly unfair. Anyone who is interested in the role of a prison governor would be well advised to read John Podmore's Book – "Out of Sight, Out of Mind."[8] It is well written and well observed on the difficult role that he performed so well for many years. He makes the point that progressively the role of governor has been undermined as Westminster and the all powerful Ministry of Justice has taken hold of the system. At a time when all other public services are embracing localism it is surprising that the Ministry of Justice is still wedded to the notion that it knows best. It is clear that there needs to be governance, audit and policy direction but for too long this has progressively swamped the hapless governor in a blizzard of red tape, inspections and attempts to catch him or her out. Podmore writes:

"During my 3 and a half year in command of HMP Brixton I counted a total of 15 audits and inspections."

Podmore goes on to describe the fate of modern prison Governors as being "a body of people that has become buried in bureaucracy." When you read his book his description almost exactly accords with the fate of many a teacher and head teacher I knew, who served under the previous government's regime for schools: drowning in dictats, changes in government plans, and always overlaced with a strong "London knows best" attitude.

Others have remarked that for such an important institution there is no staff college or ongoing training programme. You do not want to breed a bunch of clones but better training, in the company of peers, should produce better Governors. It is also a great shame that the annual governing governor's conference has been reduced and eventually scrapped down the years. As the media seek ever more sensational stories the chance for the prison governor to engage with the public, in the location where his prison is based, and the local press who cover that area, has been reduced. One of the consequences of this is to push the Governor further and further back into the bunker mentality. This discourages engagement with the wider public, or outside agencies who might have innovative ways to approach mental health, rehabilitation and so much more. The truth is that good prisons require good leadership; and that means leadership from both the bottom up and the top down. Endless bureaucracy and reorganisations help no one. A disinterested and unmotivated staff will neither help change the way the prison is nor the way in which the prisoner is reformed.

Leadership Training for Governors:
Prisons are independent, hierarchical institutions where leadership, direction and control are top down processes delivered by the governing governor. The quality of governorship varies considerable and will typically drive

the performance culture and approach of prisons. In prisons where leadership is reactive and conservative it is unlikely that there will be a culture of innovation that is required to run a modern prison that effectively addresses the rehabilitative needs of prisoners. The emphasis is more likely to be upon meeting targets, maintaining security and administering prisoners.

There is no structured training provided within the Prison Service to develop and prepare the governors of the future. Governor development is reliant upon experience gained "on the job" and attachments to headquarter organisations. In many instances career experiences will be mixed and not always relevant to preparing these men and women to govern. Again the Prison Service is one of the few major public service organisations that does not provide senior management training. The Armed Services invest heavily in preparing its leaders for senior command positions. The training is designed to broaden experience, promote critical analysis, inspire, innovate, and develop command potential. The training is also used to identify officers with the skills and ability to hold specific command appointments and channel others in areas where their skills will be best used. There is real need for the Prison Service to identify and develop their talented governors to ensure they are equipped and best prepared for the considerable challenges of running modern and effective prisons. I suspect that the governors and prison staff would welcome such assistance and training.

Politicians
All politicians have an unhealthy interest in what commentators call "law and order". Crime figures are

bandied around at elections by all sides, and the upcoming police and crime commissioner elections on November 15th 2012 will again bring policing and criminal justice issues to the fore.

It is also true to say that many a politician has tasted life at Her Majesty's pleasure: most recently, there has been the disastrous impact of the expenses scandal, which rightly saw 4 Members of Parliament sent to prison. Most served 18 months. One of them David Chaytor, was sentenced by a judge to 18 months but was let out after just 4 and half months. He therefore served 25% of his sentence, and was then let out on "technical probation". There is little he had to do on release save not commit a crime. The public and others unsurprisingly found this abbreviation of his sentence hard to swallow.

More significant custodial sentences were handed out to the former Tory heavyweights Jonathan Aitken and Jeffrey Archer – both of whom have, since their release, become passionate prison reformers.

For my part, notwithstanding my professional background in the law, I am acutely conscious that it is a dangerous and fraught situation for any person elected to represent a community as a Member of Parliament to then decide to give the wider world the "benefit" of his views on prisons and criminal justice.

I do so with great caution, and due deference to the efforts of successive politicians who have tried to improve the service that the state provides to protect its citizens from those who have transgressed.

Prisons / Justice Minister
Clearly the job of Prisons / Justice Minister is exceptionally difficult. It is worth noting the views of the

former Governor of HMP Brixton and Belmarsh, John Podmore.

He served in the Prison Service under many Ministers including Douglas Hurd, Michael Howard, and David Blunkett amongst others. His book is compelling on the subject of politicians, prisons and the press. He wrote[9]:

"Politicians don't like prisons. Appointments to the post of Prisons Minister are punishment postings. Few come out unscathed."

Podmore's assessment continued:

"It was May 9 2007, in the panic years of the Labour government, that the most significant change took place in criminal justice administration. Prisons and Probation were moved into the Department of Constitutional Affairs, which was renamed the Ministry of Justice. The architect of this change was Dr. John Reid, who was appointed Home Secretary on 5 May 2006, replacing Charles Clarke, after the latter was removed in the wake of a Home Office scandal involving the release of foreign prisoners.

Storming into the Home Office like a Celtic supporter heading for the last pie in the shop, Reid's academic standing was based on a doctoral thesis listed on Stirling University's website as: "Warrior Aristocrats in Crisis: the political effects of the transition from the slave trade to Palm Oil Commerce in the Nineteenth Century of Dahomey."

Podmore added that his attempt to obtain a copy of this thesis never proved successful. He added:

"Reid held 8 government posts in the space of 7 years, running three of the government's largest departments in the space of just 2 years, Health and Defence, before the Home Office. When he became Secretary of State

for Health, he is reported to have said, "Oh No. Not Health." When he joined the Home Office and took on the responsibility for prisons I heard one senior colleague say: "Oh No. Not John Reid."

At the Home Office Reid hit the ground running. He rushed around condemning his predecessors as incompetent and his staff as dysfunctional. His famous description of the department as "not fit for purpose" became part of the new bureaucratic lexicon. Morale in Reid's department hit rock bottom as it wrestled with a new leader whose loyalty was to the next election rather than a genuine improvement in his department. He would have been better to have done a PhD on leadership and management rather than obscure elements of the Kingdom of Dahomey."[10]

It is clear Mr Podmore was not impressed by Dr Reid. All I can say is that it is a brave man who is Prisons Minister....

"In my country we go to prison first and then become President."
Nelson Mandela

Part One

The Holy Trinity

It is all very well describing who you would like to run a prison and tinkering with the provider of the service but, in truth, you will never turn around prisoners unless you address the holy trinity:

• Drugs
• Literacy
• Work

I analyse these three problems in detail below. Some of what I write is new. Some of it is reminder of best practice that has sadly not been actioned for decades because of disinterest, lack of innovation, money or skewed priorities. I offer some basic but effective ideas that have simply been ignored in the last 20 years. It is also fair to say that two years into the coalition government's approach steps are being taken to address the failings that have existed for years.

However, if we are serious about turning round the 85,000 regular prisoners these are three key problems we must address.

The full detail is set out below, but roughly

• 50% of prisoners have a drug problem,
• 50% of prisoners cannot read write or do basic maths

and

• 66% of prisoners were out of work before committing the crime for which they were sent to prison.
• Half of all prisoners lack the skills required for 96% of jobs and only one in five are able to complete a job application form.

Can we be surprised that they reoffend?

Chapter 2

A Drug Free Prison?

"The degree of civilization in a society can be judged by entering its prisons."
Fyodor Dostoevsky, 19th Century Russian novelist and the original author of Crime and Punishment

In the early stages of my career as a barrister in the 1990s, on a wet Monday morning, I had to go to a London Magistrates Court to represent a young man arrested on a Saturday night for attempted burglary. My client had been in police custody without drugs for over 36 hours. He almost certainly had not had any drugs on the Saturday either – hence why he was arrested for committing car crime as he sought money for drugs. Whether he liked it or not he was detoxing – known as going "cold turkey" in the trade. He was not a pretty sight. I did not need to be a doctor to recognise that he was probably a heroin addict. He was pale, withdrawn, with sallow skin, and a haunted look. The posters do not lie – Heroin does more than mess you up. This young man was violent, all but deranged, hyperactive, demanding and desperate.

He demanded I get him some drugs. I remember the conversation well – he grabbed me by the arm with a desperate urgency and said – "I just need a bit of puff [cannabis] to tide me over". Obviously I refused.

He then demanded I get him bail: we both knew his purpose was so that he could get outside and get some money, by any means necessary, and get a fix of heroin. As he was my client, I was required to ask for bail.

Predictably, and quite rightly, he was refused bail and remanded into custody. That Monday morning the Stipendiary Magistrate running the court realised that my client, the defendant, would only re-offend for more drugs if he was let out pending his trial. He could see my client's record, the offence he was arrested for, and the tell-tale signs of an addict. The offence of trying to steal a car radio was serious, but it was also the offence of choice of all drug addicts who knew they could get £25 for the stolen radio – this equating in the 1990s to the cost of a decent drugs fix.

I once met a client who admitted he had stolen over 150 car radios over 6 months for his drug habit. He was a one man crime spree around Swindon. By way of an aside, the reason that car crime has gone down is that the car makers have now made it much harder both to break into a car and steal the contents. The old days of a clothes hanger down the side of the car window and theft of your pull-out car radio / tape player in less than 30 seconds are thankfully long gone.

The tragedy is that the fact that the defendant was remanded into custody used to lead to a controlled detoxing away from heroin: my client would have been able to obtain cannabis in prison but heroin was a rare commodity inside prisons in the 1990s in my experience; it takes several weeks for someone to come off hard drugs, alcohol and cigarettes. The event I describe took place in the early 1990s. Some would argue that drug abuse in prison was worse in the 1990s. No one can be absolutely sure but my experience of countless prison visits in the 1990s was that there was widespread abuse of cannabis, but far less use of the really serious class A drugs like heroin.

Sadly, the reality in 21st century Britain is that a similar defendant remanded into custody would speedily get access to class A drugs, and heroin in particular. As discussed below, even the prescribed drug substitutes, Methadone and Subutex, which are given to addicts by the prison, are both ineffective and abused by the prisons and prisoners themselves. Some prisons make real attempts to tackle the drug problem inside. The truth is that too few prisons are interested or incentivised to get rid of the drug problem that is a cancer in their systems. That government in the past has not made eradication of drug use in prisons a priority is clear – the evidence of usage speaks for itself.

For me the conclusion is clear: it is all very well teaching an inmate to read and write, count and even learn a trade, but if they are drug dependent upon release then it will be almost impossible for them to go "straight".

How bad is the prison drug problem?

Very bad is the short answer. It is an epidemic in prisons. Some might simply be using Methadone or Subutex prescriptions given as heroin or opiate alternatives by the Prison; the rest are taking illegal drugs. Some are taking both prescribed and illegal drugs. In fact, if you want access to drugs for the first time – prison is the place where you find them:

"One in five men who report using mainstream drugs, first used them in prison."

Rt Hon David Hanson MP, 2007 Minister of State for Justice / Prisons[11]

No prison or any study, however definitive it may be, can say for sure how many prisoners are drug users, but multiple studies by the Home Office and others have shown that in some prisons in excess of 50% of all prisoners are drug users. What makes this figure more disappointing is that, in isolated cases, some Prison Governors and some staff are doing little to discourage the drug use. A drugged prison tends to be a quiet prison. When a person is detoxing, whether they be in or out of prison, they are never quiet.

How do the drugs get into prisons?

Most addicts will bring drugs into prison on being sentenced to custody by wrapping the drugs in foil, a plastic bag or a condom, and then placing it in their rectum for extraction later, when on the inside. Sometimes other orifices are used, particularly by women prisoners. This will later feed the prisoners' habit and also give them something to sell, whilst inside.

Similarly, some prisoners will do an exchange of drugs when they meet other prisoners on a court visit. The other ways for drugs to get into prison are numerous: the list attached below is not exhaustive but it covers most of the problems:

• Straightforward drug supply by corrupt prison staff or official visitors

• Drugs thrown over the prison wall and collected by prisoners

• Drugs carried in by family / domestic prison visits

• Drugs in prisoners' post / possessions

There are multiple studies, and evidence, both anecdotal and established, of how drugs get into prison, but probably the best are the detailed report, *"Inside Out: How to get drugs out of prisons"*[12], written by Huseyin Djemil, and published in 2008 by the Centre for Policy Studies, and the Blakey report, *"Disrupting the supply of drugs into prisons"*[13], a report commissioned by the

Brown government. Also key to any evaluation is the report of the leading think tank, the Centre for Social Justice, which published their Report "*Locked Up Potential*" in 2009. In addition, Her Majesty's Inspector of Prisons' published annual reports which also provide excellent data and views on this issue. This study is not a repetition of the huge tomes that already address the issue, but an attempt to address the problems and identify why successive governments have failed in the past. It also looks at different ways in which we are, and could be, tackling the problem of drugs in prison.

Drug Prevention

There are two simple ways forward that need to become a priority:

• the first is to make the prevention of drugs getting into prisons a priority for government and Prison Governors. For time immemorial the Prison Governor has been almost exclusively focused on preventing people leaving prison rather than restricting drugs coming in.

• the second is to help addicts reform such that they neither need nor want drugs, whilst incarcerated.

Both are complex issues requiring effort, time, courage, commitment on all sides and a degree of thinking outside of the box. All of us know people who have tried to quit smoking or drinking alcohol. Such decisions take effort and will power, and there are often many false starts and false dawns. It is the same for drug addicts. It helps massively if no one around you lights up, drinks or does drugs.

The success of the last Labour government in stopping smoking indoors has helped thousands quit smoking. Similar comments apply to alcoholics, who have to be in a location devoid of alcohol. The same principle applies with drugs. Addicts struggle to resist temptation when they are locked up, with little constructive purpose to occupy them, and drugs being offered on a regular basis. If we do everything possible to stop the drugs getting into prisons then this will help those who either want or should be detoxing and getting clean. It will also make the prospects of long term rehabilitation much more likely.

Stopping drugs getting into prison:

Drug importation into prisons by families, corrupt prison staff or official visitors

It is sadly well known that some families and so called friends are importing drugs into prisons. Some family members secrete the drugs literally up their sleeves, or place them in anal or vaginal orifices. The more resourceful enclose the drugs in foil or a tiny plastic bag placed in the crevices of their mouths between the teeth and the cheek and then pass the drugs whilst engaged in a long kiss goodbye.

When interviewed by the Telegraph newspaper in December 2011[14], the Chief Inspector of Prisons, Nick Hardwick, gave a graphic account to a journalist of what he had recently seen:

"Mr. Hardwick described the drugs problem in prisons as a "scourge" and criticised a "fatalistic" attitude among some officers over their ability to stop it.

He said that, while it may be difficult to eradicate the problem, "eradicating it should be the goal". It was "not acceptable and deeply shocking that people come in to prison without a drug problem and leave with one".

"Your starting position has to be that it is absolutely not acceptable," he said. "Your aim should be about getting people off drugs not maintaining them. You don't allow laissez faire, you go for improvement."

He said that in two prisons he visited he was told that prisoners who had been released on license had deliberately breached their conditions so they could be recalled and take drugs back in with them. "They don't have very high aspirations some of them," he said.

In another prison visit, he said: "There was a prisoner standing up kissing his girlfriend and it looked to me absolutely obvious that something was being passed.

"So I looked at the guys on the desk and they had it all on CCTV and I said, 'Did you see that? What are you going to do about it?'

"They said, 'Oh no we can't stop them doing that [embracing], they're allowed to do that.'

"Just an outrage. When that stuff gets out on the wings, there will be intimidation, there will be bullying and trouble. There will be debts.[15]"

Official visitors / staff:

Anecdotal evidence and some prosecutions show that other official visitors sometimes cross the line as well – solicitors have occasionally been tempted to keep a key client happy by importing into prison a much needed fix / or supply, which is then handed over during a private client / lawyer conference. It is definitely the case that some importation is conducted by prison staff. Certainly, the numbers of prison staff, official visitors, and families prosecuted and sent to jail for bringing illegal drugs into prison clearly in no way equals the scale of the drug importation problem.

Prisons are a small community, no different from a large office, school or community village. Most people know what is going on and who is doing what. However, there exists a climate of "Don't ask, don't tell", whereby few will name and shame the prisoners. It is a very brave drug free prisoner who will name the guilty prison staff member, who is dealing or supplying to another drug addicted or dealer prisoner. Put simply there is little incentive to assist the prisoner in revealing what is going on, and insufficient incentive to the prison authorities, who themselves are not fighting this key issue hard enough. Some efforts have been made but there is more that can be done.

Similarly, I have prosecuted several cases where insider information as to who was dealing in or out of prison was never revealed to the police. The movies do not lie – the informant is always more afraid of the main dealer or drugs baron than he is of the police.

Efforts to combat drugs and other items entering via the prison gates:

I have visited a large number of prisons as a lawyer, visitor and MP over the past 20 years. Category A prisons are clearly different to open prisons in the extent and quantity of the searching that goes on. However, in the vast majority of non Category A prisons the searching that goes on is either limited or non-existent. Airports process millions of visitors through basic but effective security using machinery and some searching. Why do we not use a similar system to prevent the entry of drugs into a secure environment like a prison?

The Labour government commissioned the Blakey report to assist on this issue. Mr. Blakey, a former inspector of constabulary and Chief Constable of West Mercia Police, was commissioned in 2008 by the Director General of the National Prisoner Management Service, to conduct a review into the effectiveness of the Prison Service's measures for disrupting the supply of drugs into prisons, and to make recommendations for improvements. The Blakey report, "Disrupting the supply of drugs into prisons", made 10 recommendations, all of which were accepted by the government. All will make a difference. One of the key recommendations was the searching of prisoners for unlawful contraband, metal objects and mobile phones, which would then be used to coordinate drug dealing and importation from inside the jail. To do this metal detectors and Body Orifice Security Scanners (BOSS chairs) were introduced and have been used in places. A BOSS chair effectively searches for anything metallic: it is a fast, non-intrusive, inexpensive, and highly sensitive detector designed to detect metal objects hidden in body cavities. It is commonly used in prisons to scan prisoners for weapons and contraband objects hidden in anal, vaginal, oral and nasal cavities. Typical objects being found are mobile phones, razor blades, handcuff keys, paper clips, knives, and tools. It also detects metal foil, in which drugs are often wrapped.

An example of recent successes in this field is found in the successful prosecution of George Moon, who, on 28 July 2009, pleaded guilty to running a cocaine "business" from inside his prison cell. Moon, 62, was caught red handed using a mobile phone to coordinate the importation of the Class A drugs from South America. When Moon's cell was raided in November 2008, he was found with a mobile phone, a SIM card and a notebook on his bed. The notebook contained the numbers of the other members of an organised crime gang and his associate in Panama, Leo Morgan, as well as information on packages sent from Panama to the UK. The evidence showed George Moon had used the mobile phone to make hundreds of calls over a four month period from his cell. Moon was caught when the National Prisoner Management Service intercepted a package which had been sent to HMP Lindholme marked "Legal Privilege Material." Inside were two SIM cards and a quantity of heroin hidden between fake legal documents. Moon was clearly a dealer on the outside and a dealer on the inside of the prison.

The extent of this dealing inside prison and the utilisation of mobile phones to coordinate this process is massive, and has been getting progressively worse. In 2010 one answer in parliament revealed that a bare minimum of 9000 phones were seized from prisons in 2009-2010. This is obviously and was acknowledged to be a significant underestimate of the actual number.

Parliament has tried to establish the extent of the drug problem in prisons: my Conservative colleague, the redoubtable Yorkshireman Philip Davies, MP, tried by way of a written parliamentary question, shortly before the 2010 general election, with mixed results:

Philip Davies MP [Shipley, Conservative]

"To ask the Ministry of Justice how many and what proportion of illicit drug seizures within prisons was attributed to:
• sniffer dogs
• closed circuit TV
• strip searches
• intimate searches
• searches of prison cells

• police intelligence, in each of the last 5 years"

The reply was not the most helpful:

Maria Eagle MP (Ministry of Justice; Liverpool, Garston, Labour)

"Information is not recorded in the format requested and would require requests for and detailed analysis of data returns from all prisons in England and Wales. To do so would incur disproportionate costs."

Philip is nothing if not robust and resourceful, so he also asked in March 2010:

Philip Davies MP [Shipley, Conservative]

"To ask the Secretary of State for Justice if he will make it his policy to collate at national level the

• quantity and

• type of drugs seized in prisons in England and Wales"

Maria Eagle MP (Ministry of Justice; Liverpool, Garston, Labour)

"The National Prisoner Management Service (NOMS) collates the number and type of drug seizures in prisons. The number of drug seizures in prisons in England and Wales in 2008-09 is given in the following table. Many seizures are similar in appearance and where not attributable are not categorically identified by scientific analysis. Weight is not recorded and there are no plans to record it."

Drug	Number of seizures
• Heroin	776
• Cocaine	262
• LSD	3
• Amphetamines	94
• Barbiturates	11
• Cannabis	1,731
• Tranquilisers	32

- Other   2,160
- Total   5,069

These figures have been drawn from administrative data systems. Although care is taken when processing and analysing the returns, the detail collected is subject to the inaccuracies inherent in any large scale recording system. The data are not subject to audit."

Conclusion:

You could view a series of other parliamentary questions which would clearly show some degree of local knowledge of the scale of the local problem. But all prisoners report widespread drug dealing in prison and effortless breach of testing. The argument would be from the Ministry of Justice that things have got better with Mandatory Drug Testing but prisoners would, I suspect, beg to differ.

I sat down with one former prisoner who made it clear to me that they saw copious amounts of drugs in prison, wholesale dealing and some prisoners deliberately being rearrested on license so that they could go back in to prison to make more money from drug dealing inside prison. Former Prison Governor, John Podmore, conducted interviews with ex - prisoners for his book "Out of Sight, Out of Mind"[16]. The stories told in that book make it clear how serious and widespread drug dealing is in prisons.

A Pilot Project:

Ideally, I would like to see a pilot project where every person entering a prison by any gate is properly scanned or X rayed and, if necessary, physically searched – whatever their rank or station, whatever the reason for their visit.

Such a project would clearly cost slightly more than the simple [or non- existent] searches that presently go on in non category A prisons, but could clearly be justified as a pilot at the very least.

This would require no specific legislation and would be very effective in cutting the amount of drugs entering the prison by families, visitors, and corrupt staff.

Even if a pilot scheme were carried out on visiting days or on a random basis whereby every person in the prison is properly searched, regardless of rank or station.

The inconvenience and cost of such a greater security pilot would, it can easily be argued, be offset by potentially less drug crime in and out of prison and a greater chance of those entering prison detoxing and thereby not reoffending upon release. More particularly we would at least have some evidence to base a zero tolerance approach upon.

The Ministry of Justice will tell you that there is a searching policy and that efforts have been made for years to stop drugs entering prisons. The truth is that, whilst this is a very difficult job, much more needs to be done.

Drugs thrown over the prison wall and collected by prisoners

It might seem remarkable to many people that in 2012 the easiest way to get drugs into a prison is simply to throw a parcel over the wall at a prearranged time and place. But that is the case. Clearly not all parts of a prison are vulnerable in this way; but there are certain obvious and accessible spots. Some prisons have used appropriate soft netting to cover suspect areas. But surprisingly not all prisons have done this. This process of drug delivery is assisted when the prisoner inside the prison has a mobile phone and can coordinate the drop. Prisons are aware of this and the BOSS chairs are helping prevent phone access, where they are used. However, the netting of all suspect areas has to be done and done in such a way where this option is completely ruled out. This would close a significant entry point. In addition, in certain areas, CCTV focused upon possible lobbing points would also assist.

Drugs in prisoners' post / possessions and in deliveries

This is a very traditional route of entry for drugs, phones and contraband into a prison. For the criminal or drug supplier it has the value of anonymity and takes the human factor out of the equation. But prevention can still be done without any breach of human rights. I would like parcels to be searched or scanned, particularly where there is intelligence that suggests deliveries this way. There is certainly nothing contravening a person's human right to a private life under the European Convention on Human Rights to have their possessions scanned and searched in certain circumstances. We do this every day in airports and no one gets upset or criticises the procedure.

Making Drug Testing compulsory on arrival at prison and at Crown Court courthouses:

This is so obvious and fundamental that a failure to do it is bizarre. It is best to know your problems before they enter the system. At present, we do not know. We work on a voluntary basis, whereby the prisoner is asked but does not have to tell the truth on arrival at the prison. Patently many lie. Letting people into our institutions without knowing their problems is surely a form of Russian roulette, where 4 or 5 out of 10 are drug users, yet no one bothers to find out who they are as a pre-emptive strike. For the avoidance of doubt I would like to see the prisoner drug tested on arrival at a prison.

Mandatory Drug Treatment for known drug users as part of their sentence:

The flaw in the system is that drug testing and treatment to get off drugs is not mandatory for drug users. Unsurprisingly, therefore, the take-up level in this country is still depressingly low. Consequently, as it is voluntary, most drug users do not seek to get their problem addressed. If, however, a judge was able to order drug treatment and testing as part of a sentence and this was properly enforced, then we would see results. If the judge, prison and rehabilitation teams all have an interest and incentive in the outcome then the silo system disappears and the individual and collective turnaround becomes an ever greater reality.

Overview and recommendation on preventions:

Other countries have a much greater success rate at drug prevention than Britain. Singapore, parts of Australia and the USA and particularly New Zealand lead the way, and manage to keep their prisons a lot freer of drugs than is the case here. Government has to lead here and make drug prevention a top priority.

Put simply, early testing and searching before prisoners get inside the prison must take place. Efforts have been made to get the Prison Service to sit down with the

Customs / UK Borders service and learn the lessons that the Customs / UK Borders Service have acquired at airports and border entry points. The reality is that there is a lot more that could be done.

Any prison governor who is not making and taking the recommendations of the Blakey and Djemil reports as a priority in their prisons is clearly not addressing this problem of drug importation.

Intimate searches:
This is clearly a difficult issue. There is equipment that can be used to test people's body and clothing for drug residues, which has been successfully used in Australia and elsewhere.

More particularly there is the problem as to how you search for drugs placed in a prisoner's anus, normally wrapped in a condom. The UK Borders Service has a traditional remedy for this: they place a suspected smuggler in a sealed room, with a self contained toilet, and wait for nature to take its course. Eventually, the smuggler passes the condom with the drugs inside. Such a person is then prosecuted for smuggling. There is no reason why a prison could not take such an approach where information is received (or suspected) that a prisoner may be deliberately smuggling drugs into the prison.

The Mandatory Drug Testing Regime – the law of unintended consequences
The present regime is Mandatory Drug Testing [MDT]. It was prophesied as the great big advancement by the previous government and it is not working. The system is ridiculously easy to cheat or abuse.

It was previously thought that MDT would solve the problem: many would now argue that it has made things worse.

Firstly, one has to understand that MDT is conducted in the wrong way: samples are fundamentally by urine only. Such samples are easy to cheat or avoid – by switching samples, or flushing the body's system with water before the sample is taken or simply ensuring that others are chosen for testing in your place: the evidence for this is varied – I have spoken to several ex-prisoners but the best evidence of cheating is again provided by John Podmore, the former prison governor of HMP Brixton, who sets out copious evidence of ex-prisoner's ways to beat the MDT system[17].

The 2007-2008 HMP Annual Report recorded 9% positive tests, which is plainly totally incorrect[18]. Certainly, anyone who believes the evidence suggesting that only roughly 10% of prisoners are now testing positive for drugs should be tested themselves. There is not a prison governor, guard, or prisoner who would agree that only roughly 10% of the prison population take illegal drugs. That is miles off the real figure.

The testing system is also flawed and inconsistent. There should be a switch from urine tests to mouth swabs, which are much more accurate, harder to dodge. They are used by multiple other public services, like the NHS, for example, which does all its MRSA tests by swabbing. Those who have had an MRSA swab in hospital will understand how easy, quick and simple such swabs are. There is ample evidence to show that some prisons, when compiling statistics, make sure they do not do random drug tests on those whom they think might be users – because it would show that they had a drug problem in their prison – see, for example, the HMP Chief Inspector of Prisons Annual Report 2009[19].

Even worse is the fact that few prison governors are incentivised or keen to report that they have a drug problem in their prison. Because of this managers / governors play down the problem. They are also very keen to transfer illegal drug users to prescribed drugs, like Methadone or Subutex, which although a partial respite, do nothing for the essence of the problem and often make it worse, but do make their figures look better.

Heroin abuse on the up – the law of unintended consequences

In nearly two years as an MP, the biggest lesson I have learnt is that for every executive action by government there is a consequence. Often amidst all the good that government is trying to bring to a situation, there is that significant unintended consequence. So it is with Mandatory Drug Testing. Often it is the law of unintended consequences that is the most visible and disappointing result of the executive action. Traditionally cannabis was the drug of choice in prison – it is a relatively benign drug when compared to heroin and other opiates. Cannabis takes 28 days to get out of the user's system, so if you have used it in the previous 28 days you would be caught by any testing. Thus, when MDT came in, the user in prison faced a choice – change their ways or change their drug. Few will be surprised to learn that the users simply changed their drug. As a result the users started to take heroin, which only remains in the system for 72 hours, and therefore is much easier to take and avoid subsequent detection. Heroin, as countless studies show, is not a benign drug, and is highly addictive. But at least you stand less chance of being caught by MDT!

As a result, the usage of heroin in prison has clearly risen. Thus, prison is literally producing a bunch of heroin addicts, who upon discharge can and will cause mayhem. If we reformed and improved MDT the testing of all prisoners would be much better. But failure to address this will only cause more problems further down the line.

Way back in 2002 [4/10/2002] the Guardian newspaper[20] and the Insider magazine ran an article from an inmate, Peter Harris, which graphically illustrated the effect of MDT by urine. At the time, Inside Time, the leading magazine for prisoners, ran a survey that showed that heroin abuse had gone up by 70% by reason of the introduction of MDT. As always, the desire by politicians to be seen to be doing something produced the opposite effect: there is an adage in politics which is oft forgotten until too late, but it goes something like this:

"it is better to do the right thing over time, than get the plaudits now for immediate action and a policy that will later be shown to have failed."

Drug Rehabilitation in prisons

I believe this is an absolute priority, and a fundamental reason why prison should work: you have the inmate captive. You can turn them around. You can use the fact of detention not just as a punishment, but as a basis for a fresh start in a drug-free world. Some prisons do this to great effect. Indeed, it is not difficult to find a whole series of great programmes and practices being used around the country. Much progress has been made over the past five years, and the Integrated Drugs Treatment System [IDTS] is and was a success. There are clearly lots of courses available. Individual examples of successful programmes are numerous – the Rehabilitation of Addicted Prisoners' Trust [RAPt] 12 step programme is based on an American model, and really works. The work done by the Dedicated Drugs Courts and ground breaking individual prisons, as identified in various Chief Inspector of Prisons Reports show that the country does have beacons of excellence at tackling drugs in prison that everyone in this country could emulate. Slowly the evidence is that the sporadic successes are being extended across the country.

Drug-free wings
The strongest motivation to become drug free will always come from the individual prisoner themselves. Very few ever quit smoking if they do not want to do so. The whole concept of a "drug-free wing" might be an anachronism, but the reality of drugs in prison is impossible to ignore and we have to address the ongoing problem. There should be places where a prisoner can go specifically if he does not want to be around users or dealers in drugs. Once that choice is made, it is far easier to abstain and reform. It is also far more likely that the prisoners who have chosen to go on such a wing will then report abuse in their presence. You will also have that rare and wonderful thing in a prison – a group or community of prisoners signed up and eager to change.

Previous reports by the HM Chief Inspector of Prisons [2008][21] have identified prisons where such an environment and such a change in approach can have great success:

"It was therefore noticeable that at Grendon, the only prison that is wholly a therapeutic community, MDT rates were zero. We noted that prisoners themselves actively

contributed to supply reduction measures as they valued a safe and drug-free environment. Similarly, at Askham Grange women's open prison, drug use was low, in a positive environment where women themselves wanted to remain drug free."

Drug free wings are clearly the way forward – where an individual prisoner takes control of their destiny and works collaboratively with other prisoners to ensure that there is no temptation.

Looking at overseas models, the CSJ Report, *Locked up Potential*[22], describes in detail the success of the AVE Fenix Drug Rehabilitation Programme:

AVE Fenix Prison Drug Rehabilitation Programme
Mexico and Belize

"One of the world's most successful prison rehabilitation programmes is the AVE Fenix Project which has been running for several years in Chihuaha Prison, Mexico, Cuernavaca Morelios prison, Mexico and Belize City Prison, Belize.

The course consists in each of these jails of taking 50 prisoners nearing the end of their sentences into an isolation wing for twelve weeks where they go through a disciplined regime of abstinence, physical exercise, life coaching and emotional and spiritual counselling. The prisoners on the course are not allowed visitors for the first six weeks and the last three weeks of the twelve week course. They are then released from prison into half way house accommodation where they are trained in simple employment trades or disciplines such as baking bread, cleaning, working in kitchens etc. At the end of the eighteen weeks they have completed the entire course and are free.

The training and tuition costs of the course are US$1,300 per prisoner although the state prison system continues to meet their food and accommodation costs. The re-offending rates for prisoners on these courses are 13 per cent from those released from Chihuaha prison, 14 per cent from Belize prison, and four per cent from Cuernavaca prison. Both the Mexican and Belize prison authorities praise and pay for these courses which were devised by Raymundo Leal."

In December 2008, the leading prison observer and commentator, Ron Nikkel, President of the Prison Fellowship International wrote, [as reproduced in the CSJ Report]: "without doubt the AVE Fenix programme is one of the most effective and innovative rehabilitation programmes I have ever seen during my work with NGOs in more than 110 countries. It is a model rehabilitation programme with great potential for use in other nations"[23].

The use of prescribed drugs
The overriding principle of prescribed drug use in prison is a fair and medically correct principle. It is far better that an addict receives prescribed support and stabilisation than he uses some badly cut prison heroin. The alternative of going cold turkey or obtaining illegal drugs on the prison estate is not good. In my local prison in Durham, over 1 in 4 prisoners were on such drugs at my last visit. There will always be some who do need such assistance, but the substitute drug policy has totally got out of hand, and is rightly being addressed by the coalition government. That the situation was out of hand is summed up by the reply of the Health Minister, Paul Burstow, MP, to a parliamentary question on 6/9/2010:

"In 2009-10, a total of 60,067 prisoners received a clinical drug intervention. Of these, 36,323 received detoxification and 23,744 received a maintenance prescription for opioid dependency of either methadone or buprenorphine."[24]

The numbers are simply staggering.

Three key issues arise for consideration:

i). By constantly issuing prescribed drugs – Methadone or Subutex [buprenorphine] are the normal choices. Previously too little of an effort was made to address the underlying issue of drug dependence. This is now being addressed. Most prisoners, according to many unofficial reports, will also top up their prescribed supply with illegal drugs – thereby increasing their dependence.

ii). The two prescribed drugs are not only very strong, but are themselves highly addictive and disruptive. Prisons traditionally have always prescribed Methadone. Methadone is used as a heroin or morphine substitute; it can assist withdrawal or reduction from these drugs, but it itself has huge effects. It is a severe sedative, and can be used as an analgesic, which gives a good indication of its strength. Withdrawal symptoms upon sudden deprivation are often worse than heroin. More recently Subutex (known also as Buprenorphine) has been included in the prescribed drug replacement list. Similar criticisms can be made of this drug, which is often known as "Poor Man's Smack". This drug also has appalling side effects.

Both drugs come at a significant cost to the taxpayer – money that should be spent on weaning those people off drugs and preventing access in the first place.

iii). However, the most disgraceful issue is that the use of this drug has been in the past used, quite simply, to calm down the prisoners [read patients].

William Scrimshire, inmate of HMP North Sea Camp, wrote the following letter, published in the magazine Inside Time, in March 2008. The Ministry of Justice would, I stress, argue that things have changed since the dark days of the 2008 but his story provides compelling evidence of the abuse of prescription drugs[25]:

"A number of prisoners here, with no history of heroin use or any need for such a drug, are given daily doses of Subutex and Methadone. This results in people walking around like dribbling wrecks, vomiting in hallways and making living conditions almost unbearable for those of us who are not taking advantage of North Sea Camps' willing access in dispersing such drugs like candy. Eight out of ten of these prisoners are due to this prison's answer to a quiet life – issue Subutex and Methadone willingly!"

It is a dereliction of our duty to these unfortunate people that we are using such "medication" so much. Something is very wrong with the system when this is the priority. It goes without saying that any person discharged with such an addiction / habit will have minimal employment prospects, or of remaining drug free or not revisiting jail.

Conclusion on drugs

It is dismaying that for years successive governments have not taken the issue of drugs in prison with the seriousness that it deserves. This is changing, and credit must be given for the work to introduce drug free wings, drug recovery wings and developments on IDTS, but much more needs to be done.

Chapter 3

Addresing Literacy in Prisons

"He who opens a school door, closes a prison."
Victor Hugo, French Novelist.

Many a barrister will testify to the fact that *"most cases are best defended without any input from the client"*. John Mortimer's great character, the barrister Horace Rumpole is forever grumbling that *"written instructions get in the way of a good defence"*.

The sad reality, in my experience, is that very few clients were, in any event, able to give you any meaningful written instructions. Too often my clients in prison simply could not read or write. It was very humbling.

What should happen is this: every client is entitled to be asked to be shown the prosecution case in written form. This is known as Advanced Disclosure. It is a fundamental human right – to know what it is the state alleges you have done. You then take the client through the prosecution papers and obtain his version of events. His instructions are then written down and signed by the client and you then have what is known as "a written proof of evidence". This forms the basis upon which you put forward your client's case – whatever it may be, whether it is mistaken identity, alibi, self-defence or lawful entitlement.

I once went to see a client in prison to take instructions on a forthcoming matter to which he was yet to enter a plea. Like too many of the clients I defended, he was more dysfunctional than fundamentally criminal. I asked him if he had read the prosecution papers and he shrugged a little sheepishly before replying: *"I am sorry but my reading's not so good."*

We went through the case, with my reading out the specific evidence. At the end I asked him to sign the instructions and date them. He scrawled an X. I looked at him. I added in the date. The overwhelming feeling he felt was guilt at his own inadequacy. I felt embarrassment, for both of us. He had a track record of terrible parenting, abuse, care, and expulsion from school. Until you have seen total illiteracy you cannot know how much it shocks you that a system has so failed a human being, such that they have none of the basic skills that the vast majority of us in this country take for granted.

Multiple studies show that approximately half of those in prison at any one time cannot read, write, nor possess the most basic of mathematical skills[26]. Over seventy per cent of prisoners have poor numeracy.

It is not at all surprising that upon release 70% of ex-prisoners go on to re-offend and find themselves back in prison, rather than integrating into the world of work. If more prisoners left prison having acquired some modicum of literacy, they would then have the basic skills to enable them to apply and hold down a far greater scope of jobs. They would also be far more motivated to pursue a job than revert to crime. In July 2010 a 'Make Justice Work' National Enquiry published evidence that suggested that:

"Low numeracy and literacy meant that many prisoners never even thought of applying for employment on release"[27].

This is particularly true when taking into consideration the fact that 90% of male prisoners and 85% of female prisoners left school at age 15 or 16[28] and that half of the people in prison lack basic literacy skills. This produces former prisoners effectively unable to enter gainful employment and so with a high propensity to re-offend.

The causes of illiteracy are legion – but poor parenting, truancy, limited education and social breakdown are the leading culprits. But it is not stupidity on the part of a prisoner – because most people can be taught to read and write. If we do not solve this problem whilst the prisoner is incarcerated we, the taxpayer, will be the loser. In so many cases prisoners are locked into a vicious circle that, without basic literacy ability, is exceedingly difficult to escape. Previous governments simply did not try hard enough to break this cycle.

The Benefit of Literacy Courses

No one would argue with the general notion of prisoners spending their time working or learning – as opposed to sitting around idly. The taxpayer and the prisoner benefit if an illiterate prisoner spends their sentence learning how to read and write. The solution to the problem of illiteracy in prison is to use that sentence to re-educate. However, that solution is hindered by numerous problems, some of which are admittedly difficult – although far from impossible - to correct, and some which are both easy and obvious to correct. The issue is: what can be done to improve the current system of education under sentence, and address the obstacles that exist?

Problems of Course Take-Up

Re-education under sentence is one of the most productive and effective ways a prisoner can avoid re-offending. Prisons have programmes to teach basic literacy skills –

amongst other courses and work programmes. But how much is participation in these programmes encouraged? How enthusiastic are prisoners to volunteer for such programmes and in doing so swallowing their pride by admitting to their peers their illiteracy? The answers to these two questions sadly are, 'not very much at all' and 'very rarely'.

More particularly, there is a lack of incentive for the prisoner to engage in education. Prisoners are paid more to engage in work, ie cleaning or some such prison job, than they are to engage in education.

There is a lack of synergy between the individual silos of the justice process: the incentive, and then opportunity, for study available to prisoners is key. But the biggest hurdle facing the current system is summed up by this traditional damning statistic from the National Audit Office:

"Only a fifth of prisoners, with serious literacy or numeracy needs, enrol on a course that would help them"[29]

There are issues of funding here, which cannot be ignored. The Skills Funding Agency budget is limited and efforts would be needed to persuade the Department for Business, Innovation and Skills to increase the budget to enhance education for all. Delivery of skills and training is by way of the OLASS [Prisoners' Learning and Skills Service] scheme[30]. OLASS is, fundamentally, a step in the right direction. Its objective is that:

"prisoners, in prisons and supervised in the community, according to need, should have access to learning and skills, which enables them to gain the skills and qualifications they need to hold down a job and have a positive role in society".

Whether it is right that a separate government department administers such schemes – given that it is beyond the control of the Prisons Minister – is a separate issue. Something clearly needed to be done to address literacy; we cannot pretend that 20% is good enough: it doesn't matter how effective an education course is, if uptake is only 20%. That percentage needs to be far greater.

The motivation is obvious: in March 2009, the Centre for Social Justice (CSJ) suggested that studies indicated that:

"Prisoners who do not take part in any education or training during their sentence are up to three times more likely to be reconvicted on release"[31]

Steps began to improve this situation in 2011-2012. As always, with all matters in a prison, there are few easy paths. There has to be an acknowledgement of the problem of the universal instruction, however laudable such an objective is. Some would argue that in a time of limited resources this is a targeted mantra for change best devoted to those who genuinely want to learn and change.

Individual Prison Learning Plans

Shortly after a prisoner starts their sentence they should meet with an 'Prisoner Manager' who will map out a potential work and rehabilitation plan for that individual prisoner. This is a good idea, but it is not always implemented effectively enough - as the National Audit Office found:

"Only a quarter of prisoners had been subject to initial assessment. It also found that a third of prisoner learning plans were inadequate and did not specify which courses

the prisoner should enrol on. The report also uncovered a serious gap in the provision for prisoners serving short sentences''[32]

Fortunately the new OLASS contracts are beginning to address this age old problem. It is too early to assess their outcome but the Ministry of Justice should be applauded for the new steps.

Solutions from the Courts

Leaving aside the role of parenting and better education for another debate at another time, the problem of illiteracy can and should be faced earlier in the judicial journey a prisoner is engaged upon. The ideal would be if the person being sentenced would participate in literacy courses as part of their sentence. The problems I suggest can be identified and begun to be addressed in the court room, when a judge is passing sentence. There are two main changes that I believe could be incorporated into a prisoner's sentence to improve the prospect of rehabilitation: giving judges the power to impose literacy courses on sentence, and giving sentence deductions for completing literacy courses. Such an approach is radical and would need piloting. Professionals at the Shannon Trust have made the point to me that you need the inmate to be willing to engage and learn to read before he can benefit from their skills. This is accepted. Trying to teach someone who is adamant that they do not want to be taught is clearly next to impossible. But then again - surely we have to innovate and incentivise?

I suggest that if a prisoner knew that the acquisition of literacy and other or other skills would secure him an earlier release date would that not incentivise him to engage in the wonder of learning? I think it would. To fail to try would, in my opinion, equally be a crime. I consider it vital that we incentivise to address an intractable problem.

Literacy Courses as part of a Custodial Sentence

As it stands the system relies on a prisoner making the conscious decision to seek education in prison. A sentencing judge cannot impose participation on a literacy course as part of a custodial sentence (although he can as part of a community sentence), but if we are serious about cutting re-offending rates then this needs to change. For some the mere requirement of being made to go back to school is a punishment. However, we cannot reasonably expect a large enough percentage of prisoners to make that decision by themselves. Therefore, the voluntary decision to undertake a literacy course by a prisoner needs to be extended so that a sentencing judge can enforce enrolment on a literacy course - as part of a custodial sentence. This will need greater numbers of English teachers, mentors, charities and former prisoners assisting the traditional basic methods of literacy education in a prison. Such an approach is not rocket science, but some governors treat it as if it were advice from NASA.

Many charities would argue that they are actually being restricted from being able to provide the mentoring that prisoners need.

The counter argument to this is that it is already difficult enough teaching adults who volunteer to read and write as it is, so you can imagine how tough it would be teaching those who are there against their will. This can, however, be addressed, even if total resolution may be a pipe dream.

Deductions for Successfully Completed Courses

There are five main obstacles that contribute to the low take-up of education courses by prisoners:

• The embarrassment at revealing their educational inadequacies due to peer pressure and teasing

• The financial disincentive of choosing an educational course over a work course

• The fact that enrolment is voluntary

• Insufficient mentoring or encouragement by the Prison Governor, or prison staff

• Churn and transfer mid-course, and continual reassessment by multiple providers

In some prisoners, the desire to do nothing

A credible and feasible solution to countering these obstacles whilst also preventing the problems arising from judge-enforced educational enrolment is to offer a deduction on a sentence for those that complete and pass a basic literacy course. This deduction would apply solely for basic literacy courses – reading and writing. Add to this the sense of achievement that they would have and they might then seek employment and/or further education.

The literate prisoner might argue:

"Hang on – I am literate and have a skill. Why does the illiterate get an advantage and a lesser sentence than me? That is not fair?"

Some might reply that those with skills and literacy are even more culpable for being in prison, than some of the misfortunates who do end up inside with no life or other skills whatsoever. But should not prison be about equalising society and changing the individual? Surely if someone with no literacy and who is dysfunctional and drug addicted engages with the learning programmes and then acquires the necessary abilities to become a useful member of society they should be rewarded? In the absence of any other better idea I fear those that are too reluctant for whatever reason to engage with the learning process will simply slip through the net.

Under the current system, shortly after starting their sentence, an inmate should meet with prison education staff to discuss an "Individual Learning Plan"[33], where they can undertake various courses such as: bricklaying, painting and decorating, computer and technology training, in addition to a reading and writing course. The courses can differ between men and women.

The problem is that a prisoner who cannot read, and who usually does not want to reveal this to their peers, will be reluctant to undertake any course on the basis that their illiteracy will be revealed. Many will have hidden their lack of literacy for years and will be loathe to reveal it at any point – particularly in prison.

Reading, and to a lesser extent writing, are the fundamental skills required as a precursor to any further training or education or job. You cannot even be a basic labourer on a construction site without being able to read or write. As it is a fact that sentences are reduced already for good behaviour, with releases on licence, why not make such deductions for something useful?

Obstacles from within prisons

There are obstacles to literacy that exist within prisons themselves. Often prison staff and governors do not make such skills either a priority or an aim. As such rehabilitation is more difficult.

In 2010, Ofsted – which collaborates with Her Majesty's Inspectorate of Prisons to inspect learning and skills provision in prisoner institutions – remarked that:

"Five out of the twenty-seven prisons and young prisoner institutions inspected were judged to be inadequate for learning and skills this year compared with the last two years. In addition no prisons have been judged outstanding for the overall effectiveness of their learning and skills, whereas last year saw the first prison achieve this overall judgement. This profile of inspection judgements is a serious concern"[34]

As it stands those prisoners who enrol on literacy and other education courses sometimes struggle to obtain the courses that they want. Aside from anything else this is contrary to Rule 32 of the Prison Rules, which states that:

"Educational classes shall be arranged at every prison and, subject to any directions of the Secretary of State, reasonable facilities shall be afforded to prisoners who wish to do so to improve their education by training by distance learning, private study and recreational classes, in their spare time"[35]

The reality of spare time study is questionable. There are clearly barriers to the achievement of even the most willing prisoner: for example, it is difficult to educate when access to the internet and computer facilities are so limited. On this issue Former HMP Governor John Podmore's book, "Out of Sight, Out of Mind" is interesting. He certainly argues very strongly for prisoners to have access to the internet and a computer if they are to progress – given that the entire world is now functioning through Microsoft not the Bic Biro. Although safeguards would need to be put in place, we do need to think differently on this issue.

It would certainly help if a basic lack of literacy was identified as part of an overarching initial needs assessment on reception to custody.

Prison Overcrowding

Every Governor would argue, and would be right to say, that part of the problem is overcrowded prisons. As Nick Hardwick, the Chief Inspector of Prisons, put it in his April 2010 annual report:

"Prison capacity is not simply a matter of how many prisoners can be crammed into the cells - it is also a matter of whether the prison has the resources and space to do anything useful with them"[36].

It is well known that the prison population continues to increase to record highs in excess of 85,000 prisoners. This figure is double what it was in the early 1990s. Already many prisons are overcrowded, and although they are able to function, security becomes the sole focus – at the expense of rehabilitation. Yet better rehabilitation will cut re-offending, cut costs and cut prison numbers. Thus the security threat brought on by overcrowding would be lessened.

If put under pressure the Ministry of Justice would cite the review of the Prisoner Learning Making Prison Work: Skills for Rehabilitation [OLLASS 4] programme – and it is acknowledged that this is a significant step forward. This review of Prisoner Learning Making Prison Work: Skills for Rehabilitation[37] makes it clear that the government wants the reform programme to:

• *"be radical and innovative, where it is appropriate to be, in order to make a real contribution to reducing re-offending; and*

• *create the conditions that will put a focus on local influence to meet more effectively the needs of the labour market and prisoner learners."*

My view is that the innovation needs to be about incentives for prisoners and staff to change – not just about the nature and application of the individual courses.

I have previously addressed the prison officers and governors in part in the chapter – "Who Goes to Prison" – but other key points can be made.

Staff Training

Research has shown that traditionally some prison staff attitudes in Britain are disappointing. For example, in 2005, the House of Commons Education Select Committee[38] concluded that:

''Evidence from the Prison Officers' Association suggested that there was far from a learning ethic amongst prison officers''

The Committee also noted that:

''Prison Officers were not adequately trained and worked under considerable pressures''[39]

British prison officers traditionally undergo eight weeks of training before they are deemed qualified. Compare this to Norway where prison staff train for 2 years! In Norway the re-offending rate is less than 20% compared to 70% here. In Norway prison staff are much better equipped to deal with the various challenges that they face, and in Norway they subsequently have better relationships with prisoners and a better attitude towards rehabilitation. There is also, in Norway, a radically different social attitude towards prisoners, manifested in a very different sense of community responsibility for those who have offended.

It would be wrong to say that the British public do not care for what happens to someone who goes to prison. However, do we sense that it is a reflection of our British society, as a whole, that those who transgress and commit crime are part of our society and a reflection of who we, the law abiding members of public, are? I do not think so, in the main. As a result, we do not challenge how our community lapses.

This is a difficult issue, with few simple answers but try this: if we compare a society to a football team or a military unit, we would easily identify that the members of that team or unit stand or fall as a collective. If I commit a foul such that I am red carded from my local football team and they lose because they are down to 10 men I punish not only myself but also the team, and our supporters. Similarly, if one man in a team or squad takes drugs it invariably tarnishes all the team. They have a collective desire to ensure that they play by the rules and support those who are tempted to transgress. In a military unit it is drilled into soldiers that their responsibility is to everyone in that unit – not just to themselves. For an example, just watch the classic film, "An Officer and A Gentleman"[40].

The hope would be to instil in the prison officer, and the wider public, an understanding that the man or woman who committed crime and is presently languishing in a prison cell is part of their problem and their society. On this issue there is ample evidence to show that community based local prisons are clearly part of the solution.

If we can change attitudes towards rehabilitation then we are halfway to solving the problem. Given that on a day to day basis the only human contact prisoners have, aside from with their fellow prisoners, is with prison staff, then the attitude, training, empathy and approach of those staff is crucial. If staff are dismissive of re-education attempts, then prisoners will be more reluctant to take up courses to start with – let alone pass them. We aren't talking about staff physically sitting down and helping a prisoner to learn to read and write – that isn't their job - but just asking that they simply possess an understanding and encouraging attitude, and a can do mentality to assist those in their care.

Peer Mentoring in Prisons
If we are serious about cutting prisoner numbers long term, then we need to improve the training in prisons. We need more people physically to teach in prisons. Although there is some state provision, courses are largely run by volunteers and charities such as 'The Shannon Trust', who run the successful 'Toe by Toe' scheme[41]. Although they need further support they are doing a good job under the current setup. It is patently clear that the Shannon Trust, and other mentoring organisations, could do a lot more in prisons to help bring about real change.

How this works? Peer mentoring programmes such as the Shannon Trust's Reading Plan (Toe by Toe) are highly effective at both engaging disaffected prisoners and developing life skills that are central to personal development. Prisoners who have no specific learning issues can complete the reading programme in as little as four months. Peer mentoring is relatively easy to implement in prisons, is low cost and capitalises upon an under-exploited but readily available resource – willing and able prisoners. The benefits of using peer mentors to deliver rehabilitative programmes are disproportionate to the costs involved. Using prisoners to teach and support prisoners also has the benefit that prisoners are often the only people who can engage those who are disaffected and feel society has rejected them. Peer mentoring programmes such as "Rehabilitation for Addicted Prisoners Trust (RAPt), Aim Higher, St Giles Trust and Listeners are examples of charities that use prisoners and ex-offenders to mentor prisoners who need help to address learning, health, relational and practical issues (housing, finance etc) that will better equip them for a return to society. For the rehabilitation revolution in prisons to be fully effective it must be an inclusive and integrated process that draws upon all available resources that includes thousands of willing and able prisoners who want to bring about positive change in the custodial system and in the lives of those less fortunate than themselves.

Governors

A prison governor's contract is based primarily on security[42]: traditionally their job was to keep prisoners from escaping and from attacking one another. Failure to supervise these objectives – particularly if they recur – will result in a governor's job coming under threat. Other duties are myriad but will include: making inspections, carrying out disciplinary procedures, managing the prison budget, and meeting government targets on prisoner welfare. Rehabilitation traditionally has, not surprisingly, been far down the list of a governor's concerns in such circumstances. Governors traditionally did not get blamed for having limited interest in those prisoners under their supervision other than making sure they enter and leave their prisons in reasonable health. However, it should be noted that this is changing – albeit the change is slow. Put simply it is like turning round a big ship.

All too often past evidence has shown that education

success is overstated. The CSJ report, *Locked Up Potential*, cited the 2009 evidence of the Prison Reform Group that:

"Experts are concerned that many prison establishments exaggerate the degree of their educational success"[43]

The Restrictions of Short Sentences

There are many prisoners on short sentences who are not put on literacy courses due to the course exceeding their sentence in length. This is another consequence of the target culture. Governors do not want a failure to complete a course marked down against them, regardless of that failure being due to that inmate being released. This is absurd. Essentially it means that a criminal goes into prison for a short period of time, undergoes absolutely no programme of rehabilitation, mixes with numerous other prisoners – convicted of similar offences – and then re-enters society. This is a sure recipe for re-offending. In these cases a prisoner should be able to start a literacy course in prison and finish it on probation.

Prison Libraries:

Former prisoners argue very strongly that library access in prison is limited and that availability is limited. Several make the obvious point that all too often prison libraries are full of books on gangsters and true crime, which does not exactly send out the best message.

Conclusion

Literacy and education is one of the keys to rehabilitation. We have a captive audience. Punish the prisoner – this is right. But help him too. Teach him to read and write and do basic maths. If we do not solve this problem we only have ourselves to blame when people fall through the system or reoffend again.

Chapter 4

Making Prisoners Work

"No prisoner I know wants to sit around on their arse all day watching Jeremy Kyle and daytime TV. I never met a single prisoner who did not want to be working."
Ex – prisoner, interviewed June 2012

In July 2011 my constituency of Hexham was lucky enough to welcome the former Minister for Prisons, the redoubtable former MP, Anne Widdecombe, to speak [and strictly not to dance!] What she said struck a chord with one and all, as described by the Hexham Courant:

"Miss Widdecombe has been to 130 prisons, but all for the right reasons.

She said: "the overwhelming majority were places of profound idleness where people were locked up, doing nothing, for anything up to 23 hours a day. When they were released, they were expected to lead an industrious life."

Miss Widdecombe said:

"It's cloud cuckoo land! Around 75 per cent of these people are either completely illiterate or innumerate or wholly without qualifications. Prison is a revolving door system, because we don't equip them to do anything with their lives.

"Every single convicted person should have to spend every single week doing a full week's work – either in the prison education department or in the prison workshops or a combination of the two. And the work they do in our prisons should be genuine work. We have

all heard of the days when they used to make mail bags – well, now they make millions of socks. They produce two million socks a year, but they aren't sold to M&S and they can't be for consumption of the 85,000 prisoners alone. So where are all those socks going? That shows the utter pointlessness of prison work. There should be real work for real contractors to supply real customers and pay real wages from which real deductions can be made.[44]"

I could not agree more: you do not argue with a national treasure.

Should prisoners work?

The answer seems obvious but it is astonishing how little down the years the average inmate gets out of his cell, let alone gets the opportunity to work. An analysis of the figures follows below but the short points are that:

• *too few prisoners do any work*
• *the work that they do does little to train them for a life upon release*
• *until now none of the prisoners earnings, whilst at work in prison, has been paid back to victims or other proper causes.*

The public expects prison to be a place of punishment and rightly so. But the use of work in prison as a means of changing the inmate has too often been ignored by successive governments and Prison Governors. As a barrister and an MP I have visited many prisons, but the amount of work being done by the prisoners has always been insufficient. There is too little actual work being done and insufficient constructive courses for the prisoners to learn a trade.

Work ticks all the right boxes: it is a constructive use of

time, it gives something back to society and to the victim, and it re-educates the inmate on the harsh realities of a normal life working and without crime. Change has begun, led by the *Legal Aid, Sentencing and Punishment of Offenders Bill 2012.*

The scale of the problem

Figures show that[45]:

• *two thirds of all prisoners were unemployed in the four weeks prior to imprisonment;*
• *half of all male prisoners and 70% of female prisoners have no qualifications;*
• *one in seven prisoners has never been employed.*

Given these figures, it is unsurprising that released prisoners struggle to find employment. Unemployment can contribute to re-offending, locking prisoners into a vicious cycle. It is fairly predictable that, without other prospects, the prisoner will soon be looking for another victim. Part of prison's job must be to get the prisoner working, ideally give him a skill and also make due reparation to those against whom he has offended.

Currently, 27% of men and 13% of women enter employment on release from prison[46]. This is not enough. The reality is that:

"half of all prisoners lack the skills required for 96% of jobs and only one in five are able to complete a job application form"[47].

The present work climate

Many politicians and commentators emphasise the role that rehabilitation does, could or should play during an inmate's stay in prison. What exactly do they mean when they say this? It means that we need to focus on more conventional means of rehabilitating our prisoners: and one of these is work.

Work provides structure and a roof over our heads, and something to get up for in the morning. It also should be about much more than money. It fundamentally underpins a decent moral and law abiding society. We need to outline what role work plays in our rehabilitation procedure now, and what should and could be done to make prison work more effectively for our prisoners, our prison staff and, more importantly, the public who ultimately pay for this.

In 2005, the Home Affairs Select Committee produced a report on prison working and described prison industries as being largely '*peripheral*' to the way in which the Prison Service went about its business"[48].

Not much changed in the years that followed. In 2009 the Centre for Social Justice (CSJ) reported that only 15% of ex-prisoners polled said that prison was a '*busy*' time for them[49], whilst 44% said it was '*boring*' and 29% said it was '*easy*'. This is unacceptable. The public deserves reassurances that our prisoners are putting their time in prison to constructive use. As it stands, this has clearly not been the case for a long time. There are obvious reasons as to why the current levels of low working hours are wrong. Firstly, much of the public will feel rightly aggrieved that such a large work pool is able to survive by working a third of the average hours of the rest of the population. Secondly, and more importantly, this is a monumental waste of such precious time for a prisoner. This issue was considered on 29 June 2011 when the *Legal Aid, Sentencing and Punishment of Offenders Bill* was first debated in the House of Commons.

Anna Soubry, a former criminal barrister, and the

Conservative MP for Broxtowe, painted a damning picture in the debate when she said:

"Too many of our prisoners languish in 23-hour bang up, because they cannot get on to courses and no work for them is available. The Legal Aid, Sentencing and Punishment of Offenders Bill specifically addresses such difficulties and issues...that will mean that people in prison actually work...At the moment, prison does not work. That is why we have those reoffending rates, why prisons are awash with drugs and why so many prisoners are on 23-hour bang-up".[50]

All would agree that prison should be a place of hard work and industry.

How much time do prisoners actually spend working?

• in 2005-2006 the average working week for a prisoner was 13.3hours[51].
• in 2009-2010 it stood at just 11.8hours[52] of work a week.

This is in contrast to an average working week of 31 hours per worker in the UK[53].

Most people in full time employment would work up to 40 hours a week. Clearly some jobs, particularly in a recession, see people working more than 40 hours a week.

The 2005 Home Affairs Select Committee report *Rehabilitation of Prisoners* stated that:

"Prison industries continue to be run in isolation from other activities rather than as a complement to other rehabilitation measures...Hardly anywhere in the prison estate does the work regime yet reflect the structured working week found in outside work".[54]

70

There is no evidence that the situation improved between 2005 and 2010.

However credit where it is due - there is evidence now of a change in the Ministry of Justice's approach: on the 24th May 2012, the Ministry of Justice team launched *ONE3ONE*. Its raison d'être is to increase the work done by prisoners. The objective is for the work to be productive and useful - not just sweeping floors or digging holes in the ground, just because it is "better than sitting idle[55]"; they will be making uniforms, windows and doors, or adding value further down the supply chain.

ONE3ONE is effectively the middle man between the prison and business, winning and managing the contracts for the prisoners, both with the public and private sectors. The benefits are obvious. For businesses, they are given a quality, competitive and reliable service. Indeed, DHL's Vice President recognised the benefits, saying "Working prisoners can offer a valuable contribution to operations using their enthusiasm and intelligence. It is great experience for our managers and colleagues"[56]. The Code of Practice for Work in Prisons is set out in Appendix 1.

The hope is that the prisoner will learn how to work within a team, build their self-confidence and a CV. More importantly, they are given the opportunity to work! One ex prisoner said this:

"The print shop has given me a good background for my future prospects of employment after release. This is due to some of the excellent training by the staff and instructors. It has enabled me to undertake an NVQ qualification. It has also been a great help to my self esteem and given me pride in what I do and can achieve in the working environment"[57].

Moves to ensure that the victim gets compensation by the inmate doing work in prison

As Ken Clarke, MP, the Secretary of State for Justice, explained when introducing the *Legal Aid, Sentencing and Punishment of Offenders Act* to the House of Commons, the new Act will:

"allow us to deduct wages from prisoners so that instead of their just being a drain on the system we can deduct money to help to pay for services for the victims of crime. The Bill places a positive obligation on courts to make prisoners pay compensation directly to victims".[58]

Noting the importance of a strong work ethic in our prisons, he added:

"my reforms include, for example, introducing a 40-hour working week across the prison estate to introduce productive hard work into prisons in place of enforced idleness"[59].

Prisons down the ages have always featured some degree of work. The original starting point was the Prisons Act of 1952, which provided for work, some prisoner pay and deductions from that pay. In July 1996, Parliament enacted the Prisoners' Earnings Act (this would have permitted deductions to be made from prisoner pay. This would then contribute to victims funds, crime prevention, prison upkeep, the prisoner's own dependants, and other good causes. The government of the day would receive a small amount of tax on the earnings made). Unfortunately, the Act was not brought into force before the General Election in May 1997 and successive Labour governments put this Act on the backburner. This has now changed. The provisions of the Prisoner Earnings Act are now being implemented, by way of the Legal Aid, Sentencing and Punishment of Offenders Act 2012 [full details in the appendix at the end of this book]. This is clearly a step in the right direction. For the first time victims and the state will get some real compensation from prisoners whilst they work in prison.

These measures create a win-win situation whereby prisoners benefit from the skills that a working day brings, the public benefits from the rehabilitation positives that this brings, and the victim receives a monetary 'compensation' from the prisoner.

The previous limits on victim repayment

There was admittedly, before 2012, a compensation order system in place, although it was very ineffective. David Burrows, the Conservative MP for Enfield Southgate, pointed out in the House of Commons debate in June 2011 that the old compensation system was:

"seriously under-used. Only 18.1% of prisoners in 2010 were ordered to pay compensation"[60].

In the same debate, Mr Burrows also praised the decision to implement the Prisoner Earnings Act. Highlighting the usefulness of work schemes in prison, he said:

"We are not going to let prisoners sit idle in their cells; they will do proper work purposefully, and their earnings will go into a victims' fund...We need to ensure that there is retribution, restoration and rehabilitation. The rehabilitation revolution will go much further and deeper than simply this Bill, because it will ensure that we have payment by results...We will ensure that this is done across the country-paying people to get into work, to stop reoffending and to ensure that they get off drugs.[61]*"*

The effect of the changes

It is good that, in the future, a judge imposing a custodial sentence can instruct the prisoner to work and then pay some financial compensation to victims: this is restorative justice. It is right that prisoners should earn a monetary reward for their work, and again the importance of this continuation into outside working life cannot be stressed enough. But, and this is a word that is very rarely used when discussing prisons, prison should act as an incentive. It should incentivise the inmate to prepare for a working life as a civilian. The full text of the key section of the Legal Aid, Sentencing and Punishment of Offenders Act, on prisoner working, are set out in Appendix 2 at the end of this book.

The rehabilitative benefits of work in prison

The benefits of prison work are clear. It has been observed that:

"prisoners who participated in prison industries had statistically higher rates of employment than prisoners who did not participate, and that they earned higher wages within one year of release"[62].

The government green paper evidence report – *Breaking the Cycle: Effective Punishment, Rehabilitation and Sentencing of Prisoners*[63] made the point that:

- *51% of women ex-prisoners said that prison work had helped them to learn to work regular hours;*
- *46% said it had helped them learn to take orders from a boss;*
- *59% said it had helped them to work with other people and;*
- *52% said it had helped them take more responsibility.*

Better still, if you are employed then there is a massively reduced chance you will re-enter prison. The risk of reoffending is cut by between a third and a half[64].

The Home Affairs Select Committee pointed out in 2005[65] that employment in prison gives one a better chance of employment outside of prison. It also gives a prisoner a variety of valuable tangible and intangible skills. Discipline, time-keeping and inter-personal skills are just as important as the vocational practical skills a prisoner can learn. For a prisoner who has never experienced work before, prison offers a unique opportunity. It also allows the prisoner to learn a trade. The hope is that he will find a job that motivates him; that will make him want to work towards something he can look forward to practising for "real" once he is released.

The provisions allowing for the creation of bank accounts for prisoners are also a first step to them approaching normality and financial stability upon release.

The prisoner work scheme should operate to benefit both the prisoner and the victim. With a savings account, a prisoner can plan for the future, providing some security during the transition from prison into the community.

Damian Hinds, Hampshire East MP, in the June 2011 House of Commons debate, also referred to the importance of a sense of continuity – a sense of a bridge – between the life of an inmate and his subsequent life as a 'civilian'.

"Work by Paul Jones at Liverpool John Moore's university identifies a clear statistical link in that prisoners who leave and are then able to open a bank account, with all the things that that leads to, including work, are much less likely to reoffend."[66]

Why traditionally has there not been enough emphasis placed on work in prisons?

The potential benefits of work have simply not been allowed to take root and flourish. The Policy Exchange report *"Inside Job"* said:

"The new agenda for real work in prison needs to be distinct from the current conception of work in prison – which is often activity for activity's sake – and mainly consists of non-commercial, short-term programmes and skills courses that do not reflect the realities of employment"[67].

At present, there is *"an embedded culture in prison regimes of not working, of simply "doing time" and of purposeful activity being optional"*[68]. Traditional work in prisons has centred around *"meaningless and to a great extent, purposeless"*[69] jobs. It is accepted that any work is more beneficial to no work. However, there is great scope to use this time more effectively. The contracted use of private companies should facilitate a much more productive use of that time. But we do need to change the anti-work culture that exists in prisons.

There are a number of reasons why this culture existed in the past. One is the paucity of organisations – public, charitable or private – who were giving work to prisoners in productive work. Of the top 10,000 charities ranked by voluntary revenue, only 26 were involved in reducing reoffending in any way[70]. Meredith Niles, in the Charity Insight Essay, "Breaking the cycle" makes a very important point when he observed:

"the fact that charities supporting vulnerable children are able to raise such significant sums year after year is evidence that the public believes the statutory services to prevent these children ending up "in the system" are

insufficient. Indeed, our prisons are filled with individuals who fell through the cracks of children's services. Half of prisoners ran away from home as a child, while 27% were taken into care"[71].

Incentives for change

Save for certain exceptions, the incentives traditionally were not there for prison governors to facilitate rehabilitation through work. The overriding priority was on maintaining internal security. However, the two aims of security and rehabilitation are not mutually exclusive. Indeed an active and focused prison population is clearly much less of a risk than one which is simply 'doing time'. There is no punishment or criticism of a prison governor for high or increased reoffending rates. It is unsurprising that, in those circumstances, governors in the past chose to prioritise security. What we need is a prison system that rewards low re-offending rates – this will provide the incentive to rehabilitate our prison population.

Examples of good practice, upon which we can build

It is not all doom and gloom, however, and there are some outstanding examples of charities showing us how to rehabilitate our prisoners. The St Giles Trust *"Through the Gates"* programme offers prisoners housing, education, training and the silver bullet of prisoner rehabilitation – employment. With regards to St. Giles Trust:

"A study conducted by Frontier Economics found that the programme resulted in a net financial benefit of at least £10 for every £1 invested; proving that investing in resettlement can produce a significant financial return"[72].

The St. Giles worker patiently develops relationships

with his clients while they are still in prison and then continues the process once the prisoner leaves, helping them to settle back in society. For example, the charity has been working with 50 young gang members in HMP Rochester. The usual re-offending rate for this group is 70-75%. The rate amongst the group that St Giles Trust work with is 10%. In Monetary terms, every re-prisoner costs the state roughly £143,000[73] a year. For a group of 50 gang members, if 75% of them re-offended, this would cost the state £5,434,000. With a St. Giles re-offending rate of 10%, the hard-pressed tax payer saves £4,719,000. As long as the savings outweigh the costs, and a worker for St. Giles Trust costs £49,000, then the benefits are obvious. This begs the question, why have we not taken their lead and run with it? Why doesn't every prison up and down the country have a *"Through the Gates"* program? The research shows that the programmes save money by reducing reoffending. We invest in our children through education in the knowledge and hope that they will return that investment during their adult life. The same thinking should apply to our prisoners.

Outside prison
No discussion of the working prison is complete without telling the Blue Sky story.

Blue Sky Development and Regeneration is a:

"not-for-profit company established by the charity Groundwork Thames Valley. It was set up to give paid work to people coming out of prison, to enable them to move successfully into long-term employment"[74].

Its success is astonishing. Employing nearly 300 ex-prisoners, it has a reoffending rate of less than a quarter of the national average[75]. Blue Sky works in the recycling and grounds maintenance sectors and its staff and supervisors are all ex-prisoners. Their vision is to break the cycle of reoffending and trigger lasting social change. This is a common refrain of politicians but no organisations have managed this level of success. The company website quotes the Prime Minister, David Cameron:

"Just look at Blue Sky. It's the only company in the country where you need a criminal record to work there. That ex-prisoner may have a problem with alcohol, may be finding it hard to get a place to live, may have a child. That's at least three government departments responsible for him. At Blue Sky, he's got the focused attention of one place with the ideas and compassion to help turn his life around"[76].

This is a shining example of the Big Society at work. The only problem is that there are not enough charities dealing with prisoners. England and Wales release 90,000 prisoners per year; Blue Sky has a work force that covers just 0.3% of that.

It is hard enough for anyone to get a job on the outside. Add in a criminal conviction and employment chances greatly diminish. Ex-prisoners are caught in a Catch-22 situation; an ex-inmate is unlikely to rehabilitate without a job, and is more likely to find himself back in prison if he doesn't find one. The Department for Work and Pensions has concluded that *"for about half of vacancies, employers are likely to reject most people with a criminal record"[77]*. With the work that they do in this sector, charities like Blue Sky are the 'leg-up' that prisoners need.

Conclusion

There are successful and cost effective work initiatives that have existed in some of our prisons in the past. The problem has always been that there were far too few of them, and they were sporadically implemented. Where they existed and were pursued they produced excellent results. Successive governments have assumed that longer sentences, harsher laws and tough prison conditions will keep our country safe. We need to think about what we want to see from any prisoner we release. We need a prisoner to be more beneficial to society when released, not less. One of the most fundamental problems with our system is that it churns out ever more dysfunctional prisoners. Traditionally, the way a prisoner's time is used harms his chances of rehabilitation – this cannot be right. Fortunately it is an approach that has had its day. The future will see work as a fundamental to both the time spent in prison and the way in which we turn a prisoner around.

The last word on the need for work

There are successes are out there. I could not finish without including this wonderful letter by the Town Clerk of Kirkham in Lancashire, to the Daily Telegraph, on the 30th July 2011:

Prisoners at work

DEAR SIR – Ted Shorter (Letters, July 28) writes of prisoners' idleness. Kirkham and the rural Fylde in Lancashire have an excellent working relationship with HMP Kirkham, which does not believe in idleness.

Rather, we are in very grateful receipt of a regular workforce to tackle every job possible, including grounds clearance and maintenance, decorating the community centre, maintaining street furniture and spot litter picking.

Very importantly, in the worst of the winter weather, they have come out to clear the pavements of snow and ice for residents and businesses, not only in the town but also around doctors' surgeries and sheltered housing schemes.

The prison makes top-quality garden furniture and sells produce from the home farm at the prison shop. The prisoners are a pleasure to work with.

M. D. Barnes
Town Clerk
Kirkham, Lancashire[78]

Hopefully in the future all prisons will be as useful as Kirkham. Certainly the Legal Aid, Sentencing and Punishment of Prisoners Bill will:

• ensure that our prisons are a place of work and industry, with innovative schemes like One3One coming into existence this summer.

• create a greater emphasis on rehabilitation to ensure prisoners leave prison with more skills than when they entered.

• Ensure genuine, and enhanced, compensation to victims;

Part Two

What type of Prison do we want?

Chapter 5

The Big Society Prison

Don't Waste A Good Crisis

*"You don't ever want a crisis to go to waste;
it's an opportunity to do important things that you
would otherwise avoid."*
Rahm Emanuel, chief-of-staff to President Barack Obama, 2008

Why can't you have a Charity running a Prison or a Church / Community coming together to take charge and turn around low-grade prisoners?

Consider this:

If Hospitals can be transformed by Foundation status, then why cannot a prison?

If educational charities like Absolute Return for Kids [ARK] or the Harris Foundation can run state comprehensive schools open to all, then why could they not run a prison?

We let private companies run our prisons, and they do a good job. However, I see no reason why a charity with by and large altruistic motives cannot also decide to take on the responsibility?

Alternatively, why can't a church or religious group run a prison?

In truth, there is no reason why these things could not happen. It's just that no one has ever really tried before. Inside prisons there are literally thousands of not for profit organisations working and producing real results.

A local overview as a template

In Hexham, in Northumberland, where I live, and where I am lucky enough to be the MP, hundreds of volunteer groups, partnerships and charitable organisations have taken over the running of a huge number of community services. Let me give a few examples.

Community Action

In Humshaugh, in my constituency in Northumberland, the community is showing it is far better at running the former post office, village shop, and pub. The Countryside Alliance and the Daily Telegraph have twice made the village shop their North East Village Shop of the Year[79]. The state allowed the post office to close and the village assets to wither away. The community has transformed them. Their scope is now extending such that this group of 60 volunteers see few limits to their new enterprise.

Similarly, the local Hexham Community Partnership[80], in my home town in Northumberland, has branched out far beyond the remit of most community partnerships: it helps to run a truly innovative regeneration project at Number 28 Derwent Road, Hexham.[81] It also runs the local cinema, and has now started to try and take over the way in which energy is provided to the town of Hexham. It has worked with other local community groups like Transition Tynedale to begin the process of harnessing the hydro power of the River Tyne, which flows through Northumberland. The aim of the Hexham Hydro Project[82] is to provide renewable hydro-electric power to significant numbers of their local townsfolk. There are innumerable other organisations locally taking on functions that would traditionally have been state run.

Recently, on the Northumberland / Cumbrian border, the town of Alston is working on the local provision of the ambulance facilities that rural areas need, but the state is struggling to provide. The project aims to establish an ambulance service for the Alston area, which would be run by a community group and staffed by local volunteers. The idea developed following proposals to close the town's current ambulance service. Local people have come together and decided to take over the service as a social enterprise, which would be utilised by the local clinical commissioning group[83].

Church based Groups

Just opened in the North East, near to Hexham, is the amazing Betel House. The Hexham Betel House is the latest one of many Betel Houses that has been established around England [there are Betel Houses in Birmingham, Nottingham, Watford, Derby and Manchester][84]. The idea started in Spain and has spread throughout Europe. In their own words these amazing homes are ground breaking at turning around people with problems:

"Betel is a group of caring, not-for-profit Christian communities in the heart of the UK dedicated to restoring homeless and long-term unemployed people to healthy, independent lifestyles. We train men and women in a wide range of life and employment skills, enabling them to rebuild a strong work ethic. All of our residences are drug- and alcohol-free and totally free of charge. We offer the opportunity of restoration to all persons who seek our help."

One cannot help but imagine what the benefits would be of a community prison. Imagine a prison run not by the public sector, or for profit. To misquote a former Prime

Minister, [the Labour Prime Minister Tony Blair] there just might be "a third way" to run a prison, in the community, by the community, and for those from that community who have fallen by the wayside. There are examples overseas: Norway has examples of community prisons, where the local community takes responsibility for those in its local prisons, and takes an active role in their resettlement and reintegration. Clearly this is not possible for a Category A top security prison but for the lower grade prisons it is more than possible.

I suggest that the debt crisis and the deficit have allowed us to look at the way the state addresses so many things. Yes the state is the ultimate provider of many public services, but why must state provision be the only way? For anyone who has spent time in prisons, their lack of innovative thought and specific engagement with the prisoner is striking. I accept that there are honourable exceptions to this general comment, but I would still like to see an aspiration status prison, like a 'Foundation Prison'. To be fair to the Ministry of Justice their competition paper makes it clear that they intend to break up the state monopoly over delivery of criminal justice services.

More particularly, I would like to see a charity run a prison, on a not for profit or relatively low profit community basis. A start would be a category D or C prison for lower risk prisoners. There are admitted problems raising capital on a not for profit format but it is not impossible. I am told that the HMP Leeds pilot attempts to get a totally new provider to run significant parts of the prison.

There are also significant difficulties and reservations by reason of law and budgets that should not be underestimated:

what accountants call "structural barriers" include the massive costs when you acquire staff whose entitlements and pensions are passed on by means of The Transfer of Undertakings [Protection of Employment] Regulations [TUPE].

Budgets are presently very focused on containment. If security and facilities management were separated life would potentially get a lot easier.

Without a "Change" Mentality, as opposed to a "Containment" mentality, very little will change.

It is not easy, that is clear. But, as a humble backbencher I thought it best to ask the Prisons Minister why this change has not happened in the past. This is not to denote criticism of any government's previous policy – I am just not sure that the Ministry of Justice has ever genuinely encouraged charities to be involved. This is the parliamentary exchange at Justice Questions in the House of Commons on March 13 2012:

Guy Opperman (Hexham, Conservative)

"What is the policy on prisons being run by a charity, and if the Minister will make a statement?"

Prisons Minister

"Charities can apply to qualify as tenders in prisons competitions, but it is unlikely that they will have the financial strength to take the legal and commercial risks of running a prison. None is on our current list of framework providers.

We are actively encouraging the participation of subcontractors, small and medium-size enterprises and voluntary and community sector organisations within the supply chain of custodial services. Fifteen such organisations attended the launch of the current round of prisons competitions."

I am allowed a supplementary question so I asked as follows:

Guy Opperman (Hexham, Conservative)

"I thank the Minister for his answer. Clearly, there are very good examples of charities working within prisons, and I urge him to work with some of them to see whether it is possible for them to take over a community-run prison that provides a local setting and a local response to prisoners' needs."

Prisons Minister

"I am obviously delighted to recognise the valuable work of charities and of the voluntary sector in supporting the rehabilitation of prisoners. It is the area of our society in which, if we can engage the voluntary sector in such work, we will find that there is significant extra capacity for people who want to do the right thing to help some of the most damaged and damaging people in society to go straight. We have to ensure that those links work and that people can do the work. As I have said, there will be concerns about whether a charity has the financial resources to underwrite the running of a prison, given the commercial and other risks concerned, but I welcome the general tenor of my hon. Friend's remarks."[85]

I came away from parliament and sat down to analyse the answers given. The truth is that no charity or community / church organisation does run a prison. Nor are they encouraged to do so. I suspect that if you would have asked 30 years ago:

Could a private company run an academy in an area of social deprivation, instead of a standard state comprehensives school? The answer would be No.

Similarly if you had suggested a foundation hospital 30 + years ago, the answer would be No.

But that still does not mean we should not analyse the Ministry of Justice's fundamental objections: the first is simply one of cost, of bank balance!

No charity would have the legal clout or money to run a prison? I do not think that will wash, as there are charities out there with very deep pockets. While I accept that we are dealing with very substantial budgetary requirements, we still need to analyse other areas where charities run very expensive projects, on behalf of or in place of the state – and actually do it a lot better.

Consider the efforts of education charities like the Harris Federation and ARK

The Harris Federation[86] comprises 13 Academies, with at least as many more planned for the future.

It specialises in providing education in the areas where the most deprived children live, and has consistently produced amazing results. They are absolute proof that the state can trust a charity to look after our children, including the finance and the running of a school.

A similar example is ARK:

Absolute Return for Kids (ARK)[87] is an international children's charity, set up in 2002, and based in the United Kingdom. ARK provides education for children in its schools in the UK, but also in the USA and India. It also has a health and child protection programme. It is innovative, successful, and a world leader in the provision of education. ARK Schools radically improve pupils' life chances; they run a network of eleven academies in London, Birmingham and Portsmouth, and close the achievement gap between children from disadvantaged and more affluent backgrounds.

The schools are non-selective, community-oriented and

are generally situated in areas of high social deprivation. Just under half of ARK Schools' pupils are on free school meals, compared with around 15% nationally.

These charities are not the only ones acting as they do, but surely when you analyse what we want from a prison system their approach to education is so very similar.

A National Prison Service:

I know that another objection to letting in an independent provider is the argument that we have a national prison service that does not allow one prison to exist in isolation from the rest. There is no doubt that this massive beast of custody throughout England and Wales is a huge creaking leviathan, into which an independent provider that I envisage would struggle to fit. But then I know similar comments were said by the Department for Education and the NHS when academies and foundation hospitals were first proposed in the last century. The Ministry of Justice and the Prison Service do not like the idea of an independent prison sitting independently outside the prison system. You can see the Ministry of Justice's point in that prisons are a different organisation to a free school, but not by much.

The reality is that this is central Westminster control, in its purest form.

I simply do not accept that it is beyond the ability of government, the Ministry of Justice and the Prison Service to allow independent providers – particularly those run on a not for profit basis, or limited profit requirement – to run a prison. They want any new provider to fit into their system. I can understand their reasons. But this argument needs to be challenged. Instead of the state requiring independent providers to fit into the state's Westminster based system, why not ask the state to make it easier for independent providers to co-exist with the state, and reverse the burden?

Are there real benefits to charitable or private organisations running a prison?

It seems to me that there is no reason why this cannot be done. In the next chapter I show how private companies have successfully taken over the state's role and now run prisons on a contracted outcome / payment-by-results basis.

It seems a short step to a prison being run:
• In a Community
• By a community charity or church based organisation
• Working on a basis where profit or cost saving is not the measure of success
• Using all the good work that charities already employ [to a limited degree when they are allowed to] in a state or privately run prison.

Surely a start would be a small local prison caring for those who have fallen by the wayside in their local community?

With the right leadership, staff, motivation, peer mentoring and a Mentality for Change a community prison could make a real difference.

Chapter 6

Prisons that Pay by Results

"However beautiful the strategy, you should
occasionally look at the results."
Winston Churchill

Do incentives work?

In my view they do. I would like all future state-funded prisons to contemplate a payment-by-results approach – I do not consider this blue sky thinking. It seems obvious that it is the way to improve outcomes, reduce reoffending, and cost the state less.

Clearly we have:
• A State Budget, and a Prisons Budget, with less money by reason of the deficit
• a rising prison population and
• strong polling that says the taxpaying public would like an improved prison service

That is a heady triumvirate of problems and expectations.

These difficult times present a golden opportunity to reshape the traditional prison system that we have. Clearly not every prison can be run by a charity or community / church. The majority will continue to exist within the aegis of the state. But the issue of who actually provides the workers in that prison is a very different thing; and on this issue the payment-by-results approach is the way forward. There is good evidence that changes are being made and the evidence in support of payment-by-results prisons is getting more and more significant.

For example, the Prisons Minister gave a speech in October 2011 outlining the changes:

"I should emphasise that payment-by-results does not in any way change our obligation to protect the public. The changes we propose to implement will not alter the fact that punishment – be it imprisonment or a community sentence - will be punitive and challenging.

Already we have pilots running at HMP Peterborough and in Greater Manchester and London. A pilot will start in October 2011 at HMP Doncaster and we are working on pilots in a public sector prison and with probation trusts."

There are a series of key questions that need to be posed and addressed:

- What is a "payment by results" prison?
- Do they get better results in terms of lower reoffending rates?
- Do they save the state money?

Are they a flagship for the future, or a warning that only the state can protect the public from criminals and reform those who can be saved or improved?

The traditional prison

You do not need to be a fan of the film The Shawshank Redemption or the TV series Prison Break to know that traditional prisons are large, rambling mostly Victorian buildings ill-adapted to the modern world and the modern objectives of custody, particularly if the raison d'etre of the prison is security, to the detriment of everything else, notably rehabilitation. If you tour these prisons you see how facilities for rehabilitation are being squeezed like a quart into a pint pot. As has been documented by successive academic reports, and multiple independent inspectorate reports, prison overcrowding severely inhibits efforts to improve behaviour and substance abuse, and to reduce reoffending.

Modern hospitals differ comprehensively to the traditional Victorian country house style hospitals. So it is with prisons: the newer prisons are being designed on different lines, with a different approach. The mindset of the Prison Governor, the staff and the key performance indicators [KPIs] that govern their approach have changed. This is where the new build prisons come into their own.

What is a prison for?

The answer is still, and will always be, that fundamentally punishment is the deprivation of liberty. The prison itself has to be a place of confinement and secure protection of the public from those inside the prison walls.

There is ample evidence to show that prisons that provide for activities, training, opportunities for rehabilitation, and reform, have much fewer problems on their wings, and are much less likely to suffer with riots and unrest than those where prisoners are locked up 23 hours a day, in cramped cells, with no opportunity to grow or change their behaviour. The statistical results on reoffending also clearly favour an enlightened approach.

Agreement that there is a place in the UK for a prison that is run by a private provider, as opposed to the state

The UK, as a whole, already has roughly 10,000 prisoners, or around 11% of its prisoner population, held in private prisons. The figure is going up – primarily because the Ministry of Justice have selected more private prisons to manage those prisons. This is a higher proportion than in the US where the figure is around 9%. Only Australia has a higher percentage of prisoners held in private prisons. This is not a new phenomenon: privatisation of prison building and then the privatisation of prison services themselves was started under the Conservative government in the 1980's and pursued with vigour by Labour in its 13 years in power. In a speech to the Prison Officers' Association in 2003, the Home Secretary, Jack Straw, MP, the Minister in overall charge of Prisons, announced that all new prisons would be privately built and run[88]. Things have gone further, with the introduction in July 2011 of the element of competition, which has been introduced to the bidding process.

What are the benefits of this private provision?

Just as rubbish collection, utilities and hospital services have been shown to have the ability to be transformed by private provision, a number of companies have shown they can run prisons better than the state.

Down the years all political parties have agreed that private provision of prison management has been beneficial to the public Prison Service. Certainly the previous government believed in enhanced private provision throughout its time in office.

In July 2004 Martin Narey, the Chief Executive of the National Prisoner Management Service, wrote to the Home Affairs Select Committee arguing that competition and private sector involvement has been critical in stimulating "radically improved performance of public sector prisons"[89].

The supporting argument is this: it is cheaper to the taxpayer, it promotes competition and better practices, and the results are potentially better.

The Prisons Minister, on the issue of payment-by-results pilots, recently said in March 2012[90]:

"The wider impact [of payment by results] will be far reaching – substantial social and economic benefits through reduced crime, and rehabilitated prisoners adopting a more purposeful and worthwhile lifestyle....paying for real outcomes is absolutely the right approach, but we do not yet know how best to make this happen. Hence our programme of pilots."

He added, on the subject of the pilot project at HMP High Down:

"this pilot will test a radically different approach, which allows us to shift the focus of the public sector onto delivery of outcomes, without needing to draw in external finance."

What is a "payment-by-results" prison?

The key aim is stopping people committing repeat crime. This is an obvious, sane and civilised objective. Ask any victim and the key phrase they repeat is that they "do not want anyone else to go through what I went through."

The key issue, and the payment trigger, is the reduction in offending, both within the prison itself and after release.

Fee structure for payment-by-results prisons

The development deal-changer for private prison providers came when governments decided to pay prisons partly by their results. At present, the majority of such arrangements are paid on a service fee or input basis. In essence, the private provider pays a fixed sum for the contracted right to run the prison, with a percentage add on that is subject to the performance of the prison.

This has started slowly under successive governments, but is rapidly being rolled out across the country. Now is the time to recognise that the old models of prisons simply do not address reoffending behaviour and build upon a positive approach to turning people around.

As this payment-by-results model improves and becomes ever more sophisticated it should be possible to structure a payment-by-results system that truly incentives the prison work force. It should be the case that the more they reform and change their prisoners, the better they are paid. Ideally, the company, the director or governor of the prison, and the prison staff are financially incentivised to try to change their prisoners' behaviour. The system should be on a basis of Key Performance Indicators that are manifestly different to the traditional public, state model. It could be argued that the present Ministry of Justice model does not go far enough, but it is a start.

Doncaster Prison Payment-By-Results Pilot Project

In October 2011 HMP Doncaster launched a new "payment by results" pilot. The prison's director, John Biggin, explained how the four-year scheme would provide innovative rehabilitation services both within the prison and 'through the gate' in the community[91].

"We know that ex-prisoners are most vulnerable in the first three months after release – they may have lost their homes and jobs and have little to return to. This is when they are most likely to reoffend, and why the support we

can provide them with is so important. Most prisoners at Doncaster are serving sentences of 12 months or less, which means that they aren't entitled to statutory support. The new pilot scheme that we're delivering on behalf of the Ministry of Justice aims to address this and offer prisoners seamless support both within the prison and, importantly, after their release.

For the duration of the pilot 10% of our annual revenue is contractually dependent on us making this work and achieving a five percentage point reduction in reoffending rates. If former prisoners end up back in court and are convicted – on any charge within a 12-month period – then our revenue is affected.

In alliance with our long-term voluntary sector and social enterprise partners - Turning Point[92] and Catch22[93] - we have designed a scheme that can be adapted to meet the specific needs of individual prisoners. To do this, the Ministry of Justice has given us the flexibility to make decisions at a local level and truly innovate to reduce reoffending. For example, we have already integrated resettlement and the prisoner management unit within the prison to provide a unique, joined-up approach to rehabilitation.

All our prisoners are now allocated a dedicated Case Manager to support them for the duration of their sentence and crucially, on release. They will offer advice and help on a range of practical matters such as employment options, housing and benefits through regular meetings at the prison and via phone calls and visits on discharge. Prisoners will also have access to a 24-hour helpline for support and guidance at any time.

We'll also ensure prisoners continue to access the wide range of programmes already on offer at the prison to reduce recidivism. These aim to provide transferable skills and qualifications that prisoners can use after they leave. For example, courses can be taken in computing, manufacturing, printing, catering and bricklaying, while drama workshops and sports aim to build confidence and a sense of self-worth.

I truly believe what we're doing here at Doncaster works and that we can achieve our targets. It will be challenging, but if we hit 5% then it's estimated that more than 15,000 further offences a year could be avoided. When you take into account the time and money spent on each prisoner by the police, the courts, probation, and the NHS if they are abusing drugs, not to mention the support services required to help victims of crime, this will deliver significant cost savings to the government, as well as much wider social benefit in terms of a reduction in crime."

Who are the Private Providers?

The examples worldwide, and in the UK, are numerous, but Doncaster is run by Serco Custodial Services, which is part of Serco Worldwide, a large multinational company. Serco has four adult prison institutions in the UK, plus a Young Prisoners Institution and a Secure Training Centre for juveniles. In addition, Serco operates two prisons in Western Australia (including the delightfully named Acacia Correctional Centre) and provides non-custodial services in Germany. Serco Custodial Services has operated Doncaster Prison and Young Prisoners Institution since it opened in June 1994. But its remit has expanded. On 31 March 2011, Serco was awarded a further 15-year contract, worth £250 million, to operate the prison on a "payments-by-results" basis until 2026.

As a result, HMP Doncaster was examined in detail, and supported, by the Think Tank, The Reform Group[94], in May 2011, as part of their assessment of private provision of public services.

An innovative approach

Studies show that HMP Doncaster goes out of its way to promote collaborative working and innovation. It has identified local external partner organisations in the Doncaster area. This partnerships programme has reached out to a wide variety of external organisations, many of which now provide courses and academies within the prison itself.

• The prison has a partnership with the Central School of Speech and Drama, which provides an applied theatre programme designed around prisoners confronting their offending behaviour.

• Similarly, professional sports clubs, such as Doncaster Rovers FC, Featherstone Rovers RLFC and Yorkshire Cricket Club all run academies inside the jail.

• The emphasis on the strong involvement of the local community is crucial: if a community is engaged, then the prisoner becomes the community's issue and problem to solve.

• The "Through the Gate" scheme, matches prisoners being released to a volunteer mentor to help the transition back into the community.

Positive prison environment

HMP Doncaster has made the creation of a positive prison environment a key feature of its efforts to reduce reoffending and improve outcomes. A concerted effort has been made by prison management to reduce unnecessary security infrastructure and ensure staff show a high standard of care towards prisoners. This includes the removal of virtually all electronic security and open consultation with staff about changes to the operational strategy. Prisoners on education, skills, and work programmes are occupied from 9 am to 5 pm to simulate a working day.

A Family First initiative has also been developed, removing security from family visiting to create a family friendly environment. This includes a room specifically for fathers to be with their partners and babies in order to reinforce family relationships during custody. An estimated 45 per cent of prisoners lose contact with their families during custody.

HMP Doncaster's strict approach to violent behaviour has also led to substantial success in ensuring the establishment is a safe environment for prisoners and staff alike. 61% of prisoners reported never feeling unsafe within the prison and the prison has achieved reductions in the victimisation and intimidation of prisoners against both local prison comparators and previous surveys.

Improved staff-prisoner relationships

A key feature of HMP Doncaster, at variance with many other prison establishments, is the good relationship between staff and prisoners. In 2010, HM Inspector of Prisons, Nick Hardwick, wrote that –

"Prisoners themselves reported positively on the way staff treated them; we saw good staff-prisoner relationships and first names were commonly used. We saw excellent staff-prisoner relationships in the segregation unit where some of the most challenging and troubled prisoners were held"[95].

The Independent Monitoring Board has argued that the work of segregation staff *"should be recommended for best practice"[96]*.

Reduced drug and alcohol abuse
It was estimated in 2007 that 80 per cent of incoming prisoners to HMP Doncaster had committed crimes related either directly or indirectly to drugs, due to a prevalent drug culture within the local area. However, the zero tolerance approach and an effective Integrated Drug Treatment System (IDTS) have significantly reduced substance abuse within the prison.

Moreover, drug levels are at an historic low within HMP Doncaster, with reductions of one third [when compared to the government target] of prisoners recording positive on mandatory tests.

The success of the Zero Tolerance campaign was recorded by the Independent Monitoring Board of the prison, which noted[97]:

"with the success of the Zero Tolerance campaign prisoners are now reaping the benefits of remaining drug and violence free".

Does it save the state money?
In addition to delivering improvements in service quality and innovations to reduce the risk of reoffending, HMP Doncaster has realised substantial savings for the taxpayer. Although direct comparability between prisons is difficult due to variations in profiles, HMP Doncaster consistently ranks among the lowest costs for male local prisons in terms of cost per place and cost per prisoner.

In addition, figures released by the Minister of Justice reveal that Serco Custodial Services successfully reduced the operational cost of HMP Doncaster year-on-year since 2007 (See below table).

Annual overall expenditure at HMP Doncaster, 2007-10

Source: Crispin Blunt MP (2011), House of Commons, Written answers and statements, 3 May 2011[98]:

Year	Overall expenditure (£):Cost per place	Overall expenditure (£): Cost per prisoner
2009-10	43,937	30,302
2008-09	44,026	30,504
2007-08	46,437	31,572

This trend continues post these figures.

The way ahead

For a proper overview of why Doncaster is the role model for the future the Prison Magazine, Inside Time, did a review of one of the programmes run there[99]:

" I went to Her Majesty's Prison &Young Offender Institution Doncaster to speak to some young prisoners about a three-day course in which they had participated run by Not All Bad Ltd, a company run by Richard 'Nooky' Nauyokas, who spent over 20 years in the British Army, and whose name will doubtless be familiar to many of you from his Bad Lad's Army television programme; a totally down to earth, no holds barred approach to putting wayward youths back on the 'straight and narrow', and giving them the strength of character to stay the course. Richard is convinced that children and adults need a unique and specialised manner to help them realise their true potential, and to give them a kick start his company is doing just that by working with educational and government departments. He now does the same thing in prison as on TV, with outstanding results. I am certain that he was delighted with the feedback from his latest venture at HMP Doncaster.

It will probably grate on the masses, who have been convinced by the Sun and the Daily Mail (along with a certain individual from the POA) that prisoners have it 'too soft', that twelve young men were being given the opportunity to take part in a three-day motivational course that businesses on the outside pay hefty fees to Richard's company. However, if those same people had the opportunity I did to meet five of the young men that took part they would have realised that the government would be better placing funding the course into every prison in order that Richard and his staff can run them instead of building new prisons – a point raised on more than one occasion by Mark, one of the young prisoners and a self-confessed 'bad lad' of many years standing! His testimony alone would convince the most sceptical observer.

The twelve lads had volunteered for the course without knowing what was involved; fortunately for them, they had not heeded the old adage 'never volunteer' – particularly when anything military is concerned!

On the first morning, they pitched up on the recreation area and their first task was to erect a very large army tent – with no help or instruction from the Not All Bad staff (think Ikea and treble the problem!) I will not spoil it, or give the game away about other tasks in case your prison decides to participate in Richard's approach to rehabilitation - however the end result was a group of young lads with a totally different approach and attitude to life. They were asked to put their trust in each other and were not left stranded; they were given an opportunity to achieve and they all did, wholeheartedly;

but perhaps most importantly they were given self-esteem and self-respect – pride in themselves and in their achievement.

Discipline is the mainstay of the courses and any transgression was punished by press- ups. Martin reckoned that he must have done about a thousand as he kept forgetting and putting his hands in his pockets! Even if they hadn't learnt anything they were fit!

In the outside world Not All Bad would take participants paint-balling or go-karting on the third day; obviously not an option on this particular course although I'm sure it would have been acceptable. They did, however, get a pretty unusual 'treat' for their day three – square-bashing! They were dressed for the part and a Drill Sergeant licked them into shape. Unlike many military recruits before them, they enjoyed the marching best of all and in the afternoon their families were able to come and watch the 'passing out parade' and presentation of certificates.

I spoke to Martin Neville, Mark Spencer, Henry Ballantyne, Mark Cross, and Martin Simon about their views on the course and how it affected them. This was a leap of faith on the Resettlement Dept's behalf as they had no idea what would be said to me ... they needn't have worried. The overwhelming reaction was one of achievement, something they all agreed was lacking in their lives. Mark was adamant that prisoners who had been on these courses should be monitored once they got out against the same number of prisoners who hadn't participated. He, along with the other four, was convinced that those who had done the course were far less likely to re-offend. They had been made to look hard at themselves and their attitudes, especially towards *others, in a way not even the ETS [Enhanced Thinking Skills] course had done. They were all convinced that they could go out, hold down jobs and lead normal lives. A tribute to them is that Richard admitted that he would have employed all of them. When asked what was his biggest achievement, other than staying the course, one of them said: 'seeing my parents proud of me'.*

The mainstay behind the decision to run these courses, and source the funding, is resettlement manager Brian Wreakes. I could wax lyrical about the resettlement department at Doncaster Prison and fill another page; suffice to say I met a team that really cared about what happens to prisoners who leave Doncaster. They start while they are prisoners and continue with outreach centres for those who have left; they help with housing and job issues, and are ever ready with support. Unfortunately I do not have the space to sing their praises on this occasion but one has to ask the pertinent question: if one prison resettlement department can instigate and run the programmes that they do, including sourcing funding for another ten motivation courses, why can't other prisons follow suit?

Taking part in Not All Bad's motivational days has had a far more profound effect towards rehabilitation for this group of lads. The government would be well advised to put the quarter of a million pounds it would save if only 75% of participants on one course did not re-offend towards funding these courses nationwide. Doncaster prison should be justifiably proud of their foresight; we shall be watching to see if the next ten courses booked have the same effect!"

The new type of prison

Why anyone would want to have a prison in the future that does not try to transform prisoners, as they do in Doncaster, is difficult to understand. Clearly, the state of the public finances means that there is a lack of building at present. The previous government flirted with the idea of vast Titan super prisons capable of holding thousands of prisoners at the same time. Finances and a change of approach mean that this uber – prison approach is not the route that the Prison Service is pursuing. It can only be hoped that innovative best practice models like Doncaster will not only be followed, but then expanded upon and improved. Payment-by-results and the key element of competition do make a difference.

A Note of Caution

It would be wrong not to make the point that this type of change will take time, and will have setbacks along the way. The new developing framework being pushed out by the new Ministry of Justice will suffer bumps on the road. The bidding process is not simple and the implementation process is harder. There is a balance to be struck between attracting firms who will take on the task of transforming a prisoner's behaviour, at a cost which is less than that which is presently paid by the state, with a better outcome.

The long term Payment-by-Results Model – lessons to be learnt from welfare?

It is worth commenting that, at present, in the Ministry of Justice's Prison contracting system only the contracting firm's profit element is at risk. This present model is around 90% service fee and 10% linked to outcomes.

This is a start – as has been made clear.

However, the payment-by-results model in welfare and job creation for the long term unemployed has been pioneered by successive governments for many years. Put simply, others have tried and road tested a system that has been stress tested and shows both results and the greater importance of outcomes. That welfare model now shows a system that started slowly and now is operated on a 30%, 40% and 30% split: thus, a company that takes on the responsibility for taking someone with long term unemployment is paid a basic fee of 30%, then a further 40% when they get that person a job and a bonus outcome fee when that person holds down a job for a genuinely significant amount of time. I paraphrase a huge programme in a sentence but that is the new welfare model.

Locally in Newcastle and Northumberland I have seen the successes and the transformative effect it is having on the long term unemployed. My visit this spring to the company Avanta, with its offices on the north shores of the River Tyne, was an eye opener. I spent a morning there observing and talking to Avanta employees. They were highly motivated, properly incentivised, local people working to provide men and women who had clearly fallen through the employment net and were struggling to get any job. Their success rate in transforming the lives of those who simply wanted to work but did not know how or where to get a job, and who lacked basic skills, was remarkable.

I would like the Prison Service to be more aggressive in its mode of working. It will take time. But the direction of travel is now clear, and there are blueprints for the plan. Future Prison Service model contracts should clearly be on a similar basis to those presently utilised in welfare work.

Any government serious about changing prisoner behaviour needs to look at payment-by-results type prisons, with an agenda where it is the outcome and transformation of the prisoner that is the most important issue.

"Call it what you will, incentives are what get people to work harder."
Nikita Khrushchev, Former Russian President

Part Three:

Criminal Justice Reform

Chapter 7:

Ending the "Silo System" in our Criminal Justice System

A policeman once told me of an arrest he had made. He was pleased to have taken a bad person off the street – off his turf. But his following comment depressed me:

"of course, what ultimately happens to him [the arrested prisoner] is not my problem."

In a way he is right – few arresting officers have any awareness of the outcome of the arrest they have made and have little knowledge of the sentence, the success of that sentence, or when the prisoner will be released onto the street that he patrols again, or indeed what state that released prisoner will be in. All patrol officers tell stories of meeting former detainees on the streets. The exchange normally goes like this:

"Morning Kevin. When did you get out of prison?"
"Last week."

No one has told the officer of this before. Mentally the officer starts making notes to himself. He knows that last year's problem is once again his problem this year and that probably little has changed throughout the prisoner's journey through the criminal justice system. Statistically the officer knows that the prisoner is much more likely to reoffend than not.

The reason he knows this is that statistics persistently show that prison does not stop re-offending; and he has seen it all before.

This is the first that the officer knows that potential trouble is back on his beat. He does not know if the prisoner has done drugs rehab, learnt a legitimate skill, or can now read or write. Nor does he know if he has a legitimate place to live.

This is not to criticise the officer. It is just that no one asked him what should be done to turn this prisoner around, what a good sentence would be or told him when the man was going to be his problem again. After the arrest, and any evidence he had to give at court to prove the offence, his involvement all too often effectively ceased.

And yet his further involvement could have made a big difference. In my constituency most beat officers can tell you who is committing the crime, why they are doing it, and most interestingly, which individual is going to commit crime next. Some are pretty good at identifying the likely petty and serious prisoners of the future. Schoolteachers can do the same. Quite obviously parents could too.

But when the prisoner comes to be sentenced the arresting officer's opinion is never asked for. Neither is the parents' opinion. This is merely the start of the overwhelming failure of the criminal justice and prison system – an epidemic of silo thinking. This could be addressed in a pilot project: one proposal would be for the courts in a particular area to take control of the situation and ask for such input on a regular basis. There is already a group of judges in every area of the country – these are the circuit judges who preside over our local Crown Courts. As a start those circuit judges could come together and be asked to make such a change. It would require minimal administrative input from government.

Silo Thinking

"Silo Thinking" may sound like an alien term, but it is a simple problem common to a variety of organisations. It describes a situation where branches of the same organisation don't coordinate their actions. Instead they focus on their own individual task, existing in their own little silo. An individual or branch with a "Silo Mentality" has no interest in the related functions of the organisation that are going on around them.

The problem is commonly identified in business, in expressions like:

"The left hand needs to talk to the right hand"

and in government where the search is always on for:

"joined up government".

Tabloid readers will know all too well the papers regular tirades against "jobsworths" – a creature who will do their own job but nothing more. Fortunately such employees are the exception not the norm, albeit we all know and have worked with such people. They tend to be resolutely focused on their own job, wilfully ignoring the fact that much of the work of their business consists of problems that are best tackled in a coordinated and cross-departmental fashion.

This principle can be extended to the problem of defendant management. I stress that it is not necessarily the people that are the problem, but the system that we all have to work within. The criminal justice process involves a number of stages when handling defendants. At each stage the individual who handles a defendant focuses solely on their responsibility, and then hands the defendant / prisoner on to the next individual. Successive governments down the years have caused this problem.

The individuals have little incentive, ability, or arguably

the time to influence any other stages of the process. It is unsurprising that this system discourages interest in the eventual outcome of the prisoner post release from custody by those responsible for catching, sentencing, managing, guarding or even rehabilitating him. The end result is a system with a disastrously poor record when it comes to prisoner rehabilitation.

The Ministry of Justice is the government department held accountable for the reduction of offending and their targets, yet it holds very few of the budget levers required to affect that outcome. There has to be acceptance of a shared problem and a shared outcome – particularly when housing is a matter for local authorities and jobs and welfare is one for the Department of Work and Pensions.

Silos in prisoner management
There are a number of groups and individuals who become intimately involved with the prisoner during their time in the criminal justice system:
- the victim
- the police officer who physically catches the criminal
- the police station where the prisoner is initially processed
- the senior police officer who collates and brings the case
- the Crown Prosecution Service (CPS)
- the various prosecution and defence lawyers in the case
- the Court system itself
- the sentencing judge
- the prison, or prisons, in which they are incarcerated
- the Prison Governor
- the prison officers

- those running rehabilitation courses in prison
- the education and training staff
- the Parole Board
- Post-release probation officers
- Benefits offices responsible for any housing and welfare upon release
- Post prison employers / charities
- The prisoner's family

All of these groups encounter the criminal from the period when the crime is committed until the prisoner is released back into society, and attempts to reintegrate.

It's not my problem

The reality is that there is little or no interaction between these different people. The previous government made a limited attempt to address this problem by introducing the National Prisoner Management Service [NOMS] but it has struggled to prove its worth. It has failed to prevent prisoners being handled like a parcel in a party game, handed from one stage to the next. The problem is that the system spits out an unreformed and untrained prisoner with a 70% likelihood of re-offending. Then when they re-offend they are handled in exactly the same manner, often resulting in the same outcome.

Collective Responsibility

The harsh reality is that everyone is a temporary holder or custodian of the offender, but no one takes responsibility for his outcome. Critics will rightly argue that this is the job of the individual to take charge of their life and change their ways, but we have examined in detail the myriad reasons why sometimes the individual struggles to do this.

Anyone who has spent time in prisons or Young Offender Institutions, knows that many prisoners have little awareness and minimal capability to deal with their problems. If you cannot read or write, have been in care or abused, were excluded from school, have minimal parental guidance, no skills, limited family support, have drug issues and are a convicted criminal, what likelihood is there that such an individual is going to decide suddenly that they must become a better and more complete person and citizen? Put bluntly, such individuals need help if they are going to achieve any kind of turnaround. Prison is not some punitive panacea that makes all prisoners reform by pure deprivation of their liberty.

No single individual or organisation will cause the change in the prisoner's behaviour. But the various government agencies working together and in partnership can effect dramatic change. The examples are all around us. It is just that sometimes we do not use them.

How do we break down the Silo mentality – the success of LMAPs and Community Partnerships?

Local Multi-Agency Partnerships, or LMAPs, have been a success: Magistrates in my constituency of Northumberland spoke glowingly of the partnership approach where any local problem is everyone's local problem.

Thus, if there is drug dealing or petty violence on an estate, it is not just the police's problem but the problem of the residents association, the housing association, local councillors, probation, social services and the police working together. LMAPs were introduced by the Labour government and were very successful at bringing together multiple agencies to address a problem that multiple agencies have a role in handling. In Northumberland we have seven Local Multi Agency Partnership (LMAP) groups across the county who tackle local crime / anti social behaviour in communities.

Similarly, Community Safety Partnerships (CSPs) are LMAPs that deal with local safety. They are made up of representatives from the police and police authority, the local council, and the fire, health and probation services. They were set up as statutory bodies under the 1998 Crime and Disorder Act. They also work with others who have a key role in local safety, including community groups and registered local landlords[100]. Going forward there is a case for CSPs to be given the autonomy and authority to influence decisions, to enable proper join up.

There are 310 of these bodies in England and a further 22 in Wales. They are designed to develop and implement strategies to protect local communities from crime and help people feel safe. Each authority or group contributes its own particular knowledge and expertise to ensure that issues of local concern are prioritised and addressed.

This is a system that could be applied more robustly to the criminal justice / prison system. Cutting down the culture where a criminal is viewed as a problem to be dealt with and then passed on and forgotten about should be a priority. By creating a system of pooled responsibility, progress might finally be made after having seen just how little the 'pass the parcel' approach has achieved.

The partnership approach where the problem is a shared problem clearly works. An example going forward is the Integrated Prisoner Management Programme. Instituted in April 2011, the way in which criminal justice service user's access drug and alcohol treatment services locally changed. The new service will be responsible for the co-ordination of a range of interventions designed to assist those within criminal justice services to reduce their offending and aid their recovery from drug and alcohol dependency. It will also assist this client group to access housing services, education, training and employment plus a range of additional 'wrap around' services in order to change their offending behaviour. It is a scheme designed to address specific reoffending criminals- known as PPOs [Prolific and Priority Prisoners]. These are people who are active prisoners, who are committing a very high proportion of all crime committed.

Simple ways to change the system

What follows is a simple set of initiatives that could make the system more joined up and less of a silo system.

Police Changes:

• When the prisoner is taken for assessment at the police station he is detained, interviewed and processed, but never drug tested. A drugs test should be taken by the custody team at the station to identify if the prisoner is under the influence or is a regular user. Such knowledge is vital later on. Given that around 50% of car crime and residential burglary is committed for money for drugs, knowledge of the reason for the offending is a key issue. This can also assist on assessment of bail by the court and the nature of the sentence ultimately passed by the court.

• Upon conviction of the prisoner, the senior investigating officer, or the arresting officer, should try, where appropriate, and when asked by a judge who thinks it will assist, to provide a one page report suggesting why the offence was committed. The present system relies upon the prisoner telling the probation officer, when the prisoner is willing to do so, as to why he committed the offence. Frequently the prisoner lies in such situations or simply does not cooperate. A judge is all too often sentencing blind as to the circumstances which brought about the criminal act.

• It would clearly assist if the judge knew that the prisoner was a known drug dealer, living homeless, or known to have other problems that a probation officer in a short interview before sentence may not know about.

Court changes

The role of the listing officer in effecting change is key. As a criminal barrister you soon realise that the two most important people in the court building are the court usher and the listing officer. The court usher runs the day to day running of the court and decides which case is called when. The listing officer also exists in every court centre and decides which case is tried by which judge. This particularly applies in the Crown Court where serious crimes are tried and the cases are longer. Many are the hours I spent sitting down with the local court Listing Officer, trying to identify as a prosecution barrister which judges were both available, and good at the particular case you had to try. Some judges can handle all work, but it is well known that many are better at handling a fraud, in particular, as compared to other judges. Thus, in fraud trials it was vital you had a judge who would make the time and effort to read the papers in advance, and who understood the complexities and intricacies of commercial theft. Or as one Queens Counsel put it to me once – *"Lord just give me a judge who has read the papers, does not interfere, and can count!"*

Similarly, some judges are empathetic, and properly trained, in handling the difficulty of sexual offence / children cases, or particularly robust enough to handle trials arising out of drugs wars or alleged / real police wrongdoing. A judge would counter that they are capable of trying any case, but just as in life, we all have our specialities and skill sets, which distinguish the competent from the very good.

But it is in the journey of a defendant through the court system that the Listing Officer can make the most difference. At present, save in exceptional circumstances, judges do not know what happens to the prisoner they sentence to custody, save that the defendant goes to prison. This may sound bizarre but to the judge who sentences a defendant each case is just a different name and number on a court list that he or she has to work through on sentence day. Very few cases are the result of a contested Not Guilty trial where the judge sentences the Guilty man at the end of a trial. Most judges hear a summary of the offence, read the probation report and then hear defence counsels short mitigation. Then they sentence to custody or a community sentence. But they have no knowledge as to what happens after the sentence is passed.

Even if the defendant breaches the community sentence it is seldom the sentencing judge who reassesses the case. The reason? No one makes this happens. Because no one says this should be the norm, save in exceptional circumstances, resentencing takes place by another judge.

What this breeds is a failure for the judge to be involved in the outcome. If this were a school or hospital we can be sure that the percentage of judges' community sentences that were successful would be graded and publicly known. If the judge has a physical and mental attachment to the sentence then both the judge, and the prisoner, are much more engaged.

There is no rule that this happens, but some judges do ask for regular reports from the Probation Service and demand that any breach of a community sentence is dealt with by them. But that is the exception not the rule. Its efficacy is well known when this exception does take place.

Dedicated Drugs courts
There is an example of successful judge-led community sentencing with a proven effect on the reoffending levels and these are found in dedicated drug courts.

The use of dedicated drug courts, rather than ordinary magistrate court proceedings, points to one promising solution to this present lack of continuity. The core of this model, imported from the US, is to allow prisoners with drug problems to be reviewed by the same judge, or panel of magistrates, continuously from the beginning to the end of a sentence. It also means that the results of mandatory drug tests or failures to fulfil certain requirements of a community order can be judged on a more individual basis, examining them in the light of progress achieved by a prisoner and their disposition to improve. Judge Philips, was one of the founding presiding judges in the drug court in Hammersmith and Fulham, and describes the unique innovation from ordinary court procedure:

"The big difference is we promise continuity. Everyone who is sentenced to a [community] drug order in this court is sentenced to be reviewed by this court. And the judge or bench that sentences is the one that reviews, and if it goes wrong, the judge or bench that resentences."

Drug courts have now been piloted in six areas in England and Wales, starting in 2001. A 2008 review by Matrix[101] found a relationship between continuity of a judicial bench and an offender completing a community order with a drug rehabilitation requirement. Thus, successful implementation of the drug court model was associated with a modest but detectable decrease in the likelihood of re-offending. A more recent review in 2010, conducted by the National Centre for Social Research, concluded that the drug court model *'was viewed by staff and prisoners as a useful addition to the range of initiatives aimed at reducing drug use and offending'* and that *'both staff and prisoners felt that continuity helped the relationship between prisoners and the judiciary develop.'*[102]

There is an argument over whether drug courts are a good use of taxpayer's money. The results in terms of reduced offending have not been as good as many hoped. I remain a fan, and it is clear that the individual judges believe in the idea. I believe that it is a fundamentally good thing to have judges better informed, more in control of the cases that they sentence, and more involved in outcomes. This can only improve outcomes over time.

Do the Courts and the Prison Service talk to each other?

Very rarely do they speak, let alone communicate on the outcome for the prisoner. Again the system does not encourage them to do so. The court passes the prison sentence. The prison service's traditional job has not been to reform the prisoner. No one asked it to do so. What is clear is that from the time the judge passes the prison sentence he also will have no idea as to what happened to the prisoner who was before him.

Very few judges have the time, or are even specifically asked, to spend meaningful time in prisons studying and assessing the effects of their work, after they become a sentencing judge.

Every criminal barrister I know has tried to engage the judge with the process of non-custodial sentencing and change, rather than allow the judge to divorce himself from the reality of his actions. I have heard many judges say, off duty, words to the effect: *"prison numbers are not my problem. I sentence the defendants as I find them. What happens afterwards is the government's problem."*

This is actually a reasonable view, and similar to a doctor's approach: when treating a patient in A+E a doctor does not analyse why a person is on the table before him. The doctor treats the patient as best he can. The analysis and how to avoid repeats – whether the cause be smoking, liver poisoning, glassings, or drug feuds, follows later, and is someone else's job.

Judges are the same; they take their defendant as they find him and then pass the sentence they think is right. But their involvement could and should continue.

A Barrister's Mitigation

I know that most of my colleagues who were criminal defence barristers have tried to engage judges with the wider implications of sentencing.

Set out below is the summary of a plea in mitigation I heard on behalf of a young man, who was a drug addict, and who had committed several thefts of items for money for drugs.

"Your Honour is faced with a simple choice. For the offence before you, even with the Guilty plea that my client has entered, custody is perfectly permissible. Indeed many tabloids and sentencing guidelines would advise it. The Court of Appeal would not overturn a sentence of 1-2 years imprisonment, or even probably more, for such an offence.

But, with respect, that is the easy option. You would send this man to prison, throw away the key for a period of time, and hope that the experience will change him, make him a better person, less drug dependent, and better able to be a more normal member of society.

The reality is that such a dramatic change is unlikely to happen. If I were a betting man, prison will make things worse not better. Given the availability of drugs in prison, and the problems this young man faces, his situation will get worse not better in prison. He will emerge no less capable of dealing with the problems that he, or society, faces.

I would urge you to take the option of a non-custodial sentence, coupled to community service, with intensive drug treatment to cure his addiction. That is the brave choice. This man commits crime because he is a drug addict. Non-custodial is not a soft option. It is actually dealing with the problem. The soft option is failing to deal with the problem, and turning this man around."

The Prison Governor

We have already addressed some of the problems for prison governors in previous chapters. Their fundamental ethos is detention, and ensuring an inability to escape. The Prisons do traditionally have Key Performance Indicators [KPIs] by which they are fundamentally run and assessed by the government. These targets are the yardstick by which prisons are graded. Clearly promotion and job retention for one and all depends upon a satisfactory score utilising these KPIs. Of course if the KPIs are not geared to reform and rehabilitation, then few governors will focus their time and energy on this issue.

Most prison governors will admit that prisoners with short term sentences are simply trouble. These prisoners are high risk, in that their chances of suicide, self-harm or inability to cope with prison life are significant. Consequently there is limited ability to do anything but incarcerate them for the short periods they are in the control of the governor. As a result they struggle to provide such a prisoner much prospect of rehabilitation. Even in relation to long term prisoners there is minimal interaction with the original police officer, the court, or retraining. However, some progress has been made with victims' involvement with prisoners, although this is still not a universal practice.

The Victim and Restorative Justice

The victim experiences many emotions: anger, violation, upset, sadness, and a loss of confidence in both themselves and society. Speak to anyone who has suffered a break in. They are never the same again. I have prosecuted hundreds of residential burglary cases. The victims were often the most traumatised of all the victims of crime that I met. In my experience, only non-consensual sex crime has a worst psychological effect on the victim.

The victim's initial desire is for the police to catch the criminal. This is followed by a desire for due and appropriate punishment. Being the victim of a crime stirs up the strongest of emotions, and rightly so. There are very few victims whose initial reaction is a magnanimous understanding of the criminal's reasons for offending.

Once the prisoner is caught and facing justice the attitude of the victim can change. Often when the victim begins to understand the circumstances of the crime, they change their mind-set. Consequently their desires regarding the outcome of the case change.

I have seen this happen in relation to dangerous driving cases – where the parents of a child or teenager have the tragedy of their son or daughter being knocked over and killed by a car. Some such incidents are caused by deliberately dangerous driving – for example, in attempts to evade the police. However, many dangerous or careless driving cases are caused by momentary lapses of concentration or plain stupidity. Few people get up in the morning and think, "*today I will drive my car in such a way as I will lose control or direction of my vehicle and hit an innocent passer-by or cyclist because I am tired, looking across at a map, or talking on a mobile phone, or yelling at my kids in the back of the car, while I am meant to be focusing on the road*".

Any police traffic officer will tell you it is terrifyingly easy to lose control of a car in a matter of seconds.

The parents who have lost a child will feel grief, outrage and all the understandable reactions to loss. This will be followed by a court process. Part of the court process involves Victim Impact Statements. Their introduction was a good thing because they give the court and the judge a real understanding of the effect of crime on the victim. Too often the victims are forgotten in the justice process. I have read some very harrowing statements in my time as a barrister. Judges read them every week and consequently have a good understanding of what victims are saying, and the real impact of the offence.

But at this stage in driving cases the grieving parents often have a change of heart. They have begun to understand the defendant as a human being, through the court process. They have developed an understanding of why the disaster happened. Naturally they sometimes change their views. They sometimes write to the judge asking for the defendant not to be sent to prison.

The victim is led to influence the outcome of the sentence because they comprehend why the crime was committed and they have a desire for some good to come out of the process. In dangerous driving cases the defendant would normally go to prison. Such an outcome can be avoided by the impact of the victim on the sentencing judge. Most judges and barristers will have come across letters to the courts that say in broad terms – *"the loss of our son should not be compounded by the loss of this defendant's life and livelihood. We believe that this defendant can reform and do good. Please do not send him to prison."* Certainly I have seen several examples of such a victim's view of sentencing being the changing influence in the decision of the judge.

The importance of the victim being involved cannot be overstated. Of course not all car crimes fall under this example. There are different examples of car thieves fleeing from a crime and driving dangerously. However, the driving example is an easy one because these disasters are often due to momentary inattention.

The victim has almost a more important role to play when the criminal is sent to jail. Let's suppose our criminal has pleaded Guilty to burglary.

Many prisoners blank out the fact or seriousness of their crimes: I have heard defendants say comments like, "they were wealthy and I was poor – they can afford to buy more". Once confronted with the reality of their crimes they often change these views, with remarkable effect.

Victim Impact Classes have been very successful in other countries. America has led the way in California and Iowa. These classes educate prisoners about the human consequences of crime. They impart an understanding of the victim's experience. An Iowa Department of Corrections study in 2007 provided good evidence to show that making participants understand the consequences of their actions, and then take responsibility for them, changes the prisoners outlook and prospects of reoffending.

The CSJ Report "Locked up Potential" cites with approval the effects of Restorative Justices conferences. As part of the report Sir Charles Pollard, former Chief Constable of Thames Valley Police wrote:

"Restorative Conferencing – where prisoners are brought face-to-face with their victims, often with family members, in a meeting run by a trained facilitator – is an innovation which can work particularly well in prison.

Rigorous evidence from Home Office sponsored trials showed that prisoners going through this process in prison re-offended one third less than those in a similar group who did not. And, even more importantly, crime victims who attended the meetings were generally highly supportive and glad they had done so. This is not an expensive thing to do once sound multi-agency processes are set up to do it: the study showed that for every pound spent, it saved another pound in CJS costs further down the line, and saved nine pounds in the reduced overall costs of crime to society."

The CSJ report then goes on to provide a compelling example of the role that the victim can play in the prisons process, by quoting from Peter Woolf's story, as originally published in the Rehabilitation of Addicted Prisoners Trust magazine[103]:

"Desperate for money, I burgled someone's house and I was arrested. Three months later I attended a Restorative Justice conference. Restorative Justice is about face to face meeting between the victim and the prisoner. I met two people whose houses I had burgled and they told me how they felt.

I couldn't believe it! How their relationships with their wives and children had suffered because of the anger. One man – he was a heart and lung surgeon – he was telling me his life's work on his laptop had gone – he couldn't sleep – he had to move out of his home and still wasn't comfortable. But worst of all when he was operating he couldn't get me out of his head and it was affecting his work. Suddenly he burst into tears and for the first time in my life I felt someone else's pain. That was the breakthrough.

There was an Outcome Agreement. The police officer facilitating said, 'What would you like to see happen to Peter?' They said, 'We would like Peter to do alright, to address his addiction problems, and never do this again.' I was dumbfounded and soon after joined the Rehabilitation for Addicted Prisoners Trust programme

[RAPt] at Norwich prison."

Peter Woolf graduated from the RAPT programme at HMP Norwich in 2002. He went on to work as an associate trainer at Restorative Solutions and with Prolific and Priority Prisoners in Barnet, and became a published writer.

There is good evidence to show that Restorative Justice Conferences work. They are not a soft option. They are often very emotional. They clearly assist the victim as the prisoner really gets to understand what he has done to the victim's life, in a way that a written victim impact statement could never show. It is accepted that restorative justice's success derives from a willingness of the prisoner to be engaged in the process. It is worth assessing whether Restorative Justice can be expanded from the pilot projects that have been done in the past and should become more widely available and utilised. When they work it is clear that the victim in many cases will find it easier to find closure and the prisoner will have a better understanding both of what he has done, and a greater motivation to change.

The Parole Board

Again, while the sentencing judge may decide that a criminal is dangerous, and the Governor may decide that an inmate may be suitable for a certain rehabilitation course, neither of them will have an instrumental say in the parole of this prisoner. How can it possibly be sensible that the person who makes the initial assessment of danger and requirement of a custodial sentence does not then help a panel decide whether this person still remains a danger? There still remains a disconnection between the efforts of those working to rehabilitate the prisoner, and those who ultimately decide the release.

What happens on release?

The previous government did make efforts to prevent re-offending. Despite this, in 2010, more than 96,700 prisoners sentenced for serious crimes had at least 15 convictions or cautions. This was a drastic increase compared to the figure in 2000 of 54,200[104]. Indeed, over the past decade the number of prisoners recalled to prison has more than quadrupled to 100,000[105].

The National Audit Office noted in a 2010 Review of Prisoners Serving Short Sentences that efforts within the prison system to link prisoners to support in the community were limited, and that the National Prisoner Management Service provides no guidelines as to how to develop effective relationships with local authorities and other external bodies.[106]

Once a prisoner had served enough of his sentence to be released on probation he was not required to enrol in education or training. In 2011 The Bromley Report noted that only 36% of people leaving prison went into any education, training, or employment[107]. Thankfully, this is now beginning to be addressed.

The need to link prison to probation was noted by the previous Labour government. The 2003 Criminal Justice Act was the worst of the dozens of Criminal Justice Acts the Blair / Brown government passed but it did contain interesting provisions to address the post prison bridge back to normal life. This was known as "Custody Plus". This would have allowed judges passing sentences of less than 12 months to allow part of the sentence to be served in prisons and part of it to be served in the community. Although returning to wider society is a challenge for all prisoners, the fact that those serving 12 months or less have a reoffending rate of 59%, suggests that they are a group that needs special attention[108].

Custody Plus

Under the provisions of "Custody Plus", judges would have been able to attach conditions to the part of the sentence that was served in the community. These conditions would target the factors that underlie the criminal behaviour and cause them to re-offend and would be dependent on the individual needs of the prisoner. This would have ensured the components of the community sentence were appropriate to them. If these conditions were not met by the prisoner, then the prisoner could be returned to custody. A Home Office White paper explicitly stated that:

"The supervisory part of the sentence should flow on seamlessly from the custodial one to ensure the prisoner is given the best possible opportunity of rehabilitation"[109]

The need to stress this linkage between custody and probation suggests a key shortfall that had been present in the criminal justice system. The prison and probation section of a sentence has been kept separate from one another, when an obvious benefit existed in linking them. This is a key example of Silo mentality that had been at work in the prison system for decades.

Sadly the government introduced all the disastrous elements of the 2003 Criminal Justice Act, of which sentences of imprisonment for an indeterminate length for public protection [IPPs] were the worst [see the next chapter], but failed to introduce Custody Plus.

They delayed several years, but in May 2006 the Labour government was still planning on introducing the measure. In a debate in the House of Lords in 2006 the Justice Minister, Lord Bassam of Brighton, stated:

"We estimate that, in 2007–08, 49,400 prisoners will be starting Custody Plus orders."[110]

The proposals within the act were reasonably sound, acting to discourage reoffending upon release. Unfortunately, by October 2006 the same Lord Bassam was confirming to parliament that the Custody Plus provisions would be deferred as resources were to be directed towards more serious prisoners.

"The government's decision to defer custody plus reflects the prioritisation of prison and probation resources towards more serious prisoners. Revised arrangements for the implementation of prisoner management for those sentenced to custodial sentences of less than 12 months have yet to be decided." [111]

The reality was that the Labour government had so mismanaged the prison service at this time that it was clogged up with Prisoners serving indeterminate sentences [see the next chapter] and they had overcrowding to such an extent that they let out over 50,000 prisoners early.

It had been estimated that the introduction of Custody Plus would have added at least 15% to the caseloads of the probation service. Clearly this is a considerable amount, particularly in these straightened times, with all budgets being affected.[112] Proponents of the scheme in 2004-2006 argued that the annual cost of re-offending by those imprisoned for less than 12 months was estimated to be between £7 and £10 billion per year in 2007-8[113]. Therefore there is a cost in continuing to neglect the reoffending rate of "less serious" prisoners. It is indisputable that implementing Custody Plus would have required a greater input of resources into the probation service; the budget is simply not there for such a project at the moment. However the measure had the potential to generate savings elsewhere. As always in government the Silo mentality had once again reared its head. A classic ministerial case of "Not In My Budget" prevailed, and the proposal was scrapped.

What is clear is that if the government struggled to afford Custody Plus in the boom years it is never going to happen in a recession, with budgets all being cut by 20%+; I welcome the recent review of the Probation Service and the Minster for Justice's review of community punishments this spring of 2012, which is ongoing, and the pilot community payment-by-results projects commencing in Staffordshire and Wales.

The aim of Custody Plus was correct. It sought to ensure that prisoners were closely managed on their reintroduction to wider society, rather than being released without active management. It explicitly linked two areas of the criminal justice system that are often considered separately, prisons and probation. The previous government missed a good chance to make change, when there was money in the bank. The present government's proposals address the same problem, but add in the benefit of a payment-by-results approach.

Conclusion
This chapter has highlighted multiple specific areas where breaking out of the Silo Mentality has obvious benefits.

These are limited snapshots of the kind of thinking we need. Incorporating all of the skills, expertise and knowledge of the many different bodies involved in the prisoners' transition, from offence to discharge and work, to create a coordinated approach to prisoner management must be the ultimate goal. Such a system would provide a better idea of what prisoners' needs to change and rehabilitate, how we can stop them from re-offending, what support they need (both in and out of prison) and then assist an understanding of those who ultimately do re-offend. I refuse to believe this is not capable of being significantly improved. But I suspect that others have said this before. When trying to break down a silo system it is clear that this it is not easy.

> *"A cement mixer collided with a prison van on the Kingston Bypass.*
> *Motorists are asked to be on the lookout for 16 hardened criminals."*
> Ronnie Corbett

Chapter 8:

Sentences for Serious Criminals

No study on prison reform would be complete without an attempt to address the issue of long term prisoners. The idea of protection for the public from serious criminals is quite right. If someone commits a serious crime they should and will go to jail. No one has an issue with that. The issue of how you treat serious criminals – although they are not sentenced to a life sentence is an important issue. Traditionally, such a serious prisoner received a either a long, fixed term, prison sentence, or in some rare occasions a life sentence.

The previous government attempted to address these latter types of criminals with a new sentences in 2003: their idea was the "Indeterminate sentences of Imprisonment for Public Protection" (IPPs).

What were IPPs?

The purported purpose was to detain people who posed a risk to the public until they could be rehabilitated by prisoner management. Summarising massively, the system worked like this: the prisoner would be given a minimum and maximum "tariff sentence" of custody, which equated to the term he should serve. He would be released upon completion of that maximum tariff term, but only if he had taken courses to satisfy the Parole Board that he was no longer a threat to society. If drafted properly, and with funding in place, it might have achieved its purpose.

However, this is not what happened.

The outcome of IPP sentencing and custody programme

IPPs proved to be a disaster on a number of levels. IPPs were a sentence poorly drafted, badly funded and extremely costly. Indeterminate prisoners in custody rose from 2003 to 2009 from 9% of all sentenced prisoners to 18%. There is no evidence to say that this is because there was more crime. Rightly this government has got rid of them, and created a new system of life and long term sentences, with a revised approach.

Criticism of the IPP Policy

In 2009 the head of the Prison Governors Association, Paul Tidball, lambasted the IPP policy, saying:

"There is no doubt that there is a mismatch between demand and resources. The [Labour] government has over the years promoted policies which mean considerably more use of imprisonment and yet has been unwilling, and now is unable, to provide the resources to make the sentences work.

Though the public will be relieved to know that there is no doubt that high-risk prisoners will be held in custody for as long as it takes for them to be properly assessed and rehabilitated, they will be less pleased that a shortage of resources means prisoners are being held longer than necessary at considerable expense to the taxpayer.[114]"

In December 2007, Lord Carlile[115], said in the House of Lords:

"The consequence of the IPP provision has been unpredicted, remains unpredictable, and is shocking to many."

The Criminal Justice Joint Inspectorate in 2010 branded the system as untenable:

"We consider that the present position is unsustainable. This suggests the need for a major policy review at Ministerial level. Such a review would need to consider whether the resources needed to manage these sentences properly are proportionate to the benefits they might achieve[116]."

The Prison Reform Trust was a constant and vocal critic of the system. In a joint report by the Prison Reform Trust and the Institute for Criminal Policy Research at King's College London, with the support of the Nuffield Foundation, they damned the IPP policy and system, saying:

"One of the least carefully planned and implemented pieces of legislation in the history of British Sentencing.[117]

Why was this policy of IPPs introduced?

The need to keep some of the most violent prisoners separate from the rest of society is undeniable. This was, however, not the reason why the Labour government decided to change a system that had worked reasonably well and introduce instead Indeterminate Sentences of Imprisonment for Public Protection by the Criminal Justice Act of 2003.

The reality is that there was no prisoner management, just people locked up with no prospect or opportunity for parole. The system was brought in under the then Prime Minister, Tony Blair, in early April 2005. A cynic might point out that this was on the exact day that the May 2005 general election campaign started.

Because of the drafting the courts were effectively obliged to give an IPP as a staple sentence. As a consequence within two years of their implementation the numbers sent to prison under an IPP sentence ballooned[118].

Clearly some might argue that the desire was to make the government of the day appear to the public to be tough on crime to the public. The fact is they did not think the policy through, refused to fund the necessities for the system, and failed to have a clear idea of what it was that they wanted this policy to achieve.

Subsequently the government amended the legislation in 2008, but it still mushroomed totally out of control, with ever greater numbers of prisoners being sent to prison on a totally false premise. This resulted in the farce of the previous government letting out 50,000 prisoners on short sentences early, as there was insufficient space in the prisons, rather than admitting it had an IPP prison problem.

If you are going to introduce a system which is outwardly aimed at cutting crime, then why would you not implement and fund your own system so that it works properly? I welcome the fact that the coalition government has abolished IPPs. Sadly, having initially welcomed this decision the opposition then objected to this decision, when it was announced and debated in the House of Commons in the latter parts of 2011.

IPP Prison Populations

The figures for those held in prison for public protection sentences are a clear indictment of the system and an indication that reform is urgently needed.

In 2010 the Prison Reform Trust wrote a paper describing how the IPP sentence was "unjust and unsustainable"[119]. At that time in January 2010, of the

2,468 people being held beyond tariff, 466 had completed no accredited offending behaviour programmes whatsoever[120]. In other words the government and courts had said:

• We will pass a tariff sentence on you
• We accept you could change
• We will provide you with accredited offending behaviour programmes to help you change

But in reality they simply did not provide the courses or make efforts to change these people. It was a disgraceful programme, and fundamentally dishonest of the government to behave in this way.

Upon assessing the problem it became clear that the coalition government had to do something.

At the end of March 2011, when the reform process brought about by the Legal Aid and Punishment of Offenders Act Bill began, things had got worse and there were:

• 6,550 prisoners serving IPP sentences
• 6,400 of which were male and 150 female

While this number is bad enough in its own right, the figures for those held beyond their set tariff term [eg 5 years] was more disturbing. As of March 2011 over half of the prisoners serving IPPs remained in jail past their minimum tariff. Indeed, so dysfunctional was the system that just 202 people serving IPP sentences had, at that time, been released from custody[121].

It is clear that those sentenced to an indeterminate sentence were likely to stay well beyond tariff[122]. Indeed, many people given an IPP sentence under the old 2003 legislation, subsequently amended in 2008, are still in custody.

These figures raise one fundamental question:

Why were so many of these prisoners passing their minimum tariff dates and failing to convince the Parole Board to release them under licence?

It is quite clear that the difficulty lies in prisoners being unable to show the Parole Board that they were reformed and no longer a threat to the public. These prisoners will continue to be unable to do so if their courses for rehabilitation are not provided.

Initially, Ed Miliband, the Labour party leader, and his Shadow Justice Secretary, Sadiq Khan MP, supported the proposal for reform. Sadly that changed, as they saw possible political advantage. Miliband instructed his Shadow Justice Secretary, Sadiq Khan MP, to oppose the reform. During the debate on the 1st November 2011, at the second reading of the Legal Aid and Punishment of Offenders Bill in the House of Commons I berated the Shadow Justice Secretary for his brazen turnaround as an opportunistic bandwagon came along: "The flip-flops of the shadow Justice Secretary would put a kangaroo to shame."[123]

Frances Crook, the Director of the Howard League for Penal Reform [and a former Labour party councillor] took a very dim view of both the policy, and this change in the Labour party stance. She attacked the Labour Justice Secretary, Sadiq Khan, MP, for his approach on the reform of IPPs and his decision to object to their abolition in 2011, as follows:

"Sadiq Khan expresses his view that scrapping IPPs...are somehow soft on crime. This directly contradicts the pledge given by the Labour leader, Ed Miliband, in his very first conference speech that they would be supportive of penal reform...Abolishing IPPs is not radical penal reform at all. To me it is common sense.[124]"

Even senior judges have attacked the policy. In the 2009 House of Lords case of Secretary of State for Justice v James and Lee all of the judges attacked IPPs.

Lord Hope of Craighead, in his decision, lambasted the policy but particularly the then Secretary of State:

"There is no doubt that the Secretary of State failed deplorably in the public law duty...He failed to provide the systems and resources that prisoners serving those sentences needed to demonstrate to the Parole Board by the time of the expiry of their tariff periods...that it was no longer necessary for the protection of the public that they should remain in detention.[125]"

Lord Carswell called the lack of funding 'unfathomable' and said:

"I would only add that this case provides yet another example of the problems caused by over-prescriptive sentencing legislation. The draconian provisions of section 225 of the Criminal Justice Act 2003...created entirely foreseeable difficulties when sentences for imprisonment for public protection were passed with short tariff terms. [126]"

However, the real damning verdict on IPPs came from Lord Brown of Eaton-under-Heywood. He concluded his judgement:

"I cannot, however, part from this case without registering a real disquiet about the way the IPP regime was introduced. It is a most regrettable thing that the Secretary of State has been found to be – has indeed now admitted being – in systemic breach of his public law duty with regard to the operation of the regime, at least for the first two or three years. It has been widely and strongly criticised, for example by the Select Committee on Justice. The maxim, marry in haste repent

at leisure, can be equally well applied to criminal justice legislation, the consequences of ill-considered action in this field being certainly no less disastrous. It is much to be hoped that lessons will have been learned.[127]"

Reforming a discredited, poorly managed, and underfunded system isn't being soft on crime and sentencing. It is keeping the worst prisoners from our streets, and saving those who can eventually give something back.[128]

The Coalition Government Approach

When the coalition government took office, they consulted on reforming the flawed system. In the government's 2010 green paper: "Breaking the Cycle: Effective Punishment, Rehabilitation, and Sentencing of Prisoners"[129], there were the first steps to reforming the system.

The Ministry of Justice proposed that indeterminate sentences of Imprisonment for Public Protection be reserved for only the most serious prisoners. Additionally, it sought to reform the test, which the Parole Board applies when considering the release of prisoners, to create a more balanced approach. Fundamentally, this was to focus indefinite sentences on those who really could and do pose a risk of future harm to the public at large[130]. They made clear that life sentences were not going to be affected by the changes. However, the government re-iterated that the indeterminate sentence beyond their minimum tariff must be about what the prisoner is likely to do in the future, not what they have done in the past for which they served their tariff term in prison.

Reform of the IPP system

This is now an intrinsic part of the 'Legal Aid, Sentencing and Punishment of Offenders Act'. The old system is and was unworkable, had minimal support, was unfair on those who truly seek to reform, and was morally wrong. To leave it unchanged was simply not a viable option.

Maintaining imprisonment for life sentences will allow for the worst in society to remain behind bars, when they need to be kept there. Having tough fixed terms for the remaining prisoners will remove the moral dilemma, questions of legality, and a vast cost. At the same time, having a fully funded and comprehensive rehabilitation system will speed up the recovery of criminals to constructive members of society.

This should create a strong and sustainable system that actually produces results in rehabilitation as well as satisfying the need to keep dangerous people off the streets. It will take some considerable time to clear the backlog and improve this system but a start has been made.

Chapter 9:

Conclusion

Elizabeth Fry was the first real prison reformer in the early 19th Century 200 years ago. Because of her actions and her success as a social and prison reformer her face, and actions, have been depicted on the Bank of England £5 note since 2001. She was admired and supported by Queen Victoria and was a deeply influential Christian philanthropist. The tragedy is that many of problems of the prison service that she encountered are still with us.

Nowadays, it costs £45,000 a year to keep someone in prison. This is a huge sum, in these straightened times, and the results for an organisation that has a failure rate of roughly 70% are shocking. Many would argue, as the Sunday Times recently did, "that we could hand over the running of the prisons service to the management of the Savoy Hotel, and cut costs[131]".

There is so much that can be done with prisoners and our prisons but I hope that I have identified both the key weaknesses and the potential solutions. It will clearly not be easy.

If the Prime Minister is right to describe this country as "Broken Britain" then he, and we, as members of the law abiding majority, should look at a society that so fails in parenting and education that it turns out people who fall through the net into crime and reoffending all too easily.

There is hope, and a way forward. It is often said that the safety of the public is the first and paramount duty of government. This is true. I would also argue that how we deal with those individuals who go to prison is both our hardest test and the true measure of a civilised society.

We are in a crisis – it would be a shame to let this opportunity for real change to go to waste.

Appendices

APPENDIX 1

Code of Practice

Ministry of Justice

Ensuring Fairness: Code of Practice for Work in Prisons

Work in prisons should be delivered in a socially and economically beneficial way, with jobs in the community protected from the risk of being displaced as a direct result of unfair competition from prisons. Prisoners who work should have the opportunity to further their own rehabilitation. Work in prisons should allow for reparation to be made to society.

Work in prisons should be sought and delivered according to the principles of this Code of Practice.

• The work should deliver reparative and rehabilitative benefits and will be used as an opportunity to deliver reparation and rehabilitation funds.

• Prison work should not be operated anti-competitively.

• Prices should be set fairly and with reference to the market with no element of public subsidy.

• Opportunities to support businesses in the community should be sought.

• Work for prisoners in prison must not be used as a direct replacement for existing jobs in the community.

However, where a decision has already been taken by a third party to compete work that work can be competed fairly for.

• Prisoners should not be exploited.

• Opportunities to make prison work more like work on the outside should be sought, subject to pre-eminent interests such as security and the maintenance of good order. The work should be productive.

• Complaints should be dealt with thoroughly, fairly and transparently.

• Work in prison should be managed in compliance with all relevant regulatory standards, and be quality assured.

APPENDIX 2

Prisoner Earnings Rules, with regard to work in prisons, as set out in the Legal Aid and Punishment of Offenders Act 2012,

Section 129:

Employment in prisons: deductions etc from payments to prisoners

(1)In section 47 of the Prison Act 1952 (power of Secretary of State to make rules for the regulation and management of prisons etc), in subsection (1) omit "employment,".

(2)After that subsection insert—

"(1A)The Secretary of State may make rules about—

(a)the employment of persons who are required to be detained in secure training centres or young offender institutions;

(b)the making of payments to such persons in respect of work or other activities undertaken by them, or in respect of their unemployment."

(3)In that section, after subsection (5) insert—

"(6)Rules made under this section may—

(a)make different provision for different cases;

(b)contain supplementary, incidental, transitional, transitory or saving provision."

(4)After that section insert—

"47ARules about employment in prisons etc

(1)The Secretary of State may make rules about—

(a)the employment of prisoners;

(b)the making of payments to prisoners in respect of work or other activities undertaken by them, or in respect of their unemployment.

(2)The Secretary of State may make rules about the making, by the governor of the prison in which a prisoner is detained or the Secretary of State, of reductions in payments to the prisoner in respect of—

(a)work undertaken by the prisoner,

(b)other activities undertaken by the prisoner, or

(c)the prisoner's unemployment,

where those payments are made by or on behalf of the Secretary of State.

(3)Rules under subsection (2) may make provision, in a case where reductions are made by the governor, for amounts generated by the reductions to be used by the governor—

(a)for making payments for the benefit of victims or communities;

(b)for making payments for the purposes of the rehabilitation of offenders;

(c)for other prescribed purposes.

(4)Rules under subsection (2) may make provision, in a case where reductions are made by the governor—

(a)for amounts generated by the reductions to be used by the governor for making payments into an account of a prescribed kind;

(b)for the administration of the account;

(c)for the making of payments out of the account to a prisoner before or after the prisoner's release on fulfillment by the prisoner of prescribed conditions.

(5)Rules under subsection (2) that make provision for amounts generated by reductions to be used to make payments may provide for such payments to be made after the deduction of amounts of a prescribed description.

(6)The Secretary of State may make rules about the making of deductions from, or the imposition of levies on, payments to a prisoner in respect of—

(a)work undertaken by the prisoner,

(b)other activities undertaken by the prisoner, or

(c)the prisoner's unemployment,

where those payments are made otherwise than by or on behalf of the Secretary of State.

(7)Rules under subsection (6)—

(a)may provide for deductions to be made, or levies to be imposed, by the governor of the prison or by the Secretary of State;

(b)must provide that, if the governor makes the deductions or imposes the levies, the governor must pay amounts generated to the Secretary of State.

(8)The Secretary of State may make rules providing—

(a)for the making of payments by the Secretary of State into an account of a prescribed kind;

(b)for the administration of the account;

(c)for the making of payments out of the account to a prisoner before or after the prisoner's release on fulfillment by the prisoner of prescribed conditions.

(9)Rules under this section may—

(a)make different provision for different cases;

(b)contain supplementary, incidental, transitional, transitory or saving provision.

(10)In this section references to the governor of a prison

include—

(a)the director of a contracted out prison within the meaning of Part 4 of the Criminal Justice Act 1991, and

(b)an officer of a prison who may exercise the functions of a governor in accordance with rules under section 47 or this section.

(11)In this section—

• "prescribed" means prescribed by rules under this section;

• "prisoner" includes a prisoner on temporary release."

(5)In section 66(4) of the Criminal Justice Act 1967 (procedure applying to rules under section 47 of the Prison Act 1952), for "of the said Act of 1952" substitute "or section 47A of the Prison Act 1952".

(6)In section 127(6) of the Criminal Justice and Public Order Act 1994 (inducements to prison officers to contravene prison rules: meaning of "prison rules"), after "section 47" insert "or 47A".

(7)In section 4 of the Prisoners' Earnings Act 1996 (interpretation)—

(a)omit subsection (2) (application of the Act to England and Wales), and

(b)in subsection (3) (application of the Act to Scotland), for "In the application of this Act to Scotland" substitute "In this Act".

(8)In section 5 of that Act (short title, commencement and extent), for subsection (3) substitute—

"(3)This Act extends to Scotland only."

(9)In section 45(2) of the National Minimum Wage Act 1998 (exclusion for prisoners doing work in pursuance of prison rules: interpretation), in paragraph (a) of the definition of "prison rules", after "section 47" insert "or 47A".

(10)Before the coming into force of section 59 of the Criminal Justice and Court Services Act 2000 (abolition of power to provide remand centres), section 47(1A) of the Prison Act 1952 has effect as if it referred also to persons required to be detained in remand centres.

(11)Before the coming into force of section 61 of the Criminal Justice and Court Services Act 2000 (abolition of sentences of detention in a young offender institution, custody for life etc)—

(a)section 47(1A) of the Prison Act 1952 has effect as if the references to persons required to be detained in young offender institutions were to persons aged under 18 required to be so detained, and

(b)section 47A of that Act has effect as if—

(i)"prison" included a young offender institution, and

(ii)"prisoner" included a person aged 18 or over who is required to be detained in a young offender institution.

(12)The Secretary of State may make such payments to such persons as the Secretary of State considers appropriate in connection with measures that appear to the Secretary of State to be intended to—

(a)rehabilitate offenders,

(b)prevent re-offending, or

(c)limit the impact of crime.

(13)In making payments under subsection (12), the Secretary of State must have regard to the sums that have been made available to, or received by, the Secretary of State by virtue of rules under section 47A of the Prison Act 1952 (reductions, deductions and levies in respect of payments to prisoners etc.).

APPENDIX 3

The Statutory Basis for IPPs as per the 2003 Criminal Justice Act

In 2003, the Criminal Justice Act was passed by Parliament. This contained Indeterminate Public Protection sentences as set out under Chapter 5 of the Act, entitled *'Dangerous Prisoners'*. There were two types of indeterminate sentences[132]. These were Imprisonment for Life and Imprisonment for Public Protection[133].

Under a sentence of Imprisonment for Life a prisoner is given a minimum term that he must serve in prison. Once the prisoner has served this minimum term set by the court, the Parole Board will decide whether the prisoner can be released from prison to serve the final part of their sentence on licence in the community. This determination is made on the grounds of whether the prisoner remains a threat to the public at large. This licence will last for the rest of their life and cannot be revoked. Therefore if they are ever again deemed to be a threat they can be recalled to prison.

Under Imprisonment for Public Protection the prisoner will serve the minimum term set by the court. After this time the Parole Board, as with Imprisonment for Life, will determine whether the prisoner can be released. If they are they will be released on licence[134].

The primary objectives of Imprisonment for Public Protection sentences were outlined under section 225[135] of the 2003 CJA, namely, to detain in prison those who have, and continue to pose, a significant risk to the public through a potential for further serious offences, if released without rehabilitation. The system would allow these persons to be held until they no longer posed this or any similar risks. Section 225 of the Act sets out clearly the offences under which life sentences or imprisonment for public protection for serious offences[136] can be imposed.

In 2008 the Labour Justice Secretary, Mr. Jack Straw MP, amended the 2003 Criminal Justice Act. The reason was that the Indeterminate Public Protection sentences were coming under increased scrutiny and criticism. The administration of the time attempted to tighten up the circumstances under which an IPP could be levied. Section 225, subsection (3) of the Criminal Justice Act 2003 was altered to limit the cases of sentences of Imprisonment for Public Protection. This 2003 subsection had read:

"(3) In a case not falling within subsection (2), the court must impose a sentence of imprisonment for public protection."

This clause gave great authority to judges to impose IPPs' in a broad range of areas. The original qualifying statement on the application of the section created the ability for judges to do so, saying "This section applies where (b) the court is of the opinion that there is significant risk to members of the public of serious harm..."

The Criminal Justice and Immigration Act 2008 therefore amended the Criminal Justice Act 2003. Subsection (3) of the 2003 Act was amended by Section 13 of the Criminal Justice and Immigration Act 2008, which is set out in full below[137]. This removed some of the power previously handed to judges by mandating that the court could impose a sentence of imprisonment for public protection, only if one of two conditions were met.

• The first of these conditions was that the court may impose the IPP sentence if the prisoner had previously been convicted of another offence[138].

• The second condition, which can give the court the opportunity to impose an IPP sentence, is that the notional minimum term for the offence was at least two years.

APPENDIX 4

ASSESSMENT OF IPPS BY THE HOUSE OF LORDS IN THE 2009 LEGAL CASE OF JAMES AND LEE

In the 2009 House of Lords case of Secretary of State for Justice v James and Lee all of the judges attacked IPPs.

The cases of James and Lee dealt with the inability of prisoners serving an indeterminate sentence for public protection to prove their eventual fitness for release. The appellants were both prisoners that received indeterminate sentences. Both prisoners had been assigned short tariffs but due to the lack of opportunity to undergo the appropriate courses in prison, they were unable to prove their fitness for release after the expiry of the tariffs. In conjoined appeals, they appealed against the continuation of their detention despite the lapsed tariff period and the lack of the appropriate courses. The judges held that the prisoner's continued detention was not considered unlawful in common law nor was it considered a breach of the European Convention of Human Rights 1950 (as per Article 5(4)[139] and article 5 (1)[140] respectively).

The result of the case meant that the obligation on the government to provide full funding for these courses was limited. The end result is that these prisoners can end up wasting away, confined to their cells for up to 23 hours a day, where there is little chance and an even smaller incentive to reform and earn their freedom. While he did say that the continued detention of the appellants was technically lawful, Lord Hope of Craighead, in his decision, lambasted the policy but particularly the then Secretary of State:

"There is no doubt that the Secretary of State failed deplorably in the public law duty...He failed to provide the systems and resources that prisoners serving those sentences needed to demonstrate to the Parole Board by the time of the expiry of their tariff periods...that it was no longer necessary for the protection of the public that they should remain in detention.[141]"

Lord Carswell in his judgement called the lack of funding 'unfathomable' and said:

"I would only add that this case provides yet another example of the problems caused by over-prescriptive sentencing legislation. The draconian provisions of section 225 of the Criminal Justice Act 2003...created entirely foreseeable difficulties when sentences for imprisonment for public protection were passed with short tariff terms. Pelion was piled on Ossa when for some unfathomable reason it was decided that the new scheme would be resource-neutral and so sufficient facilities necessary for IPP prisoners to demonstrate their fitness for release were not made available. Fortunately section 13 of the Criminal Justice and Immigration Act 2008 has improved the situation materially, but it is to be hoped that future sentencing legislation will be framed in such a way as to avoid the pitfalls into which these misguided provisions fell[142]"

This would seem to be a thoroughly robust debunking of the policy. However, the real damming verdict on IPPs came from Lord Brown of Eaton-under-Heywood. He concluded his judgement:

"I cannot, however, part from this case without registering a real disquiet about the way the IPP regime was introduced. It is a most regrettable thing that the Secretary of State has been found to be – has indeed now admitted being – in systemic breach of his public law duty with regard to the operation of the regime, at least for the first two or three years. It has been widely and strongly criticised, for example by the Select Committee on Justice. Many of the criticisms are to be found in the judgements below and I shall not repeat them. The maxim, marry in haste repent at leisure, can be equally well applied to criminal justice legislation, the consequences of ill-considered action in this field being certainly no less disastrous. It is much to be hoped that lessons will have been learned.[143]"

APPENDIX 5

THE 2012 LEGAL AID AND PUNISHMENT OF OFFENDERS ACT 2012 PROVISIONS AS TO IPP REFORM

The new sentences for dangerous offenders

The *Legal Aid, Sentencing and Punishment of Offenders Act 2012* received Royal Assent on 1 May 2012. The changes to sentences for dangerous offenders are in Chapter 5 of Part 3, sections 122 to 128, and in schedule 18, with transitional provisions in schedule 19. Chapter 5 repeals provisions in the 2003 Act creating indeterminate sentences for public protection and extended sentences and replaces them with provisions for life sentences to be imposed on conviction for a second serious offence and new provision for extended sentences. None of these provisions are yet in force. When they are brought into force, they will apply to people whose offences were committed after that date.[145]

New "mandatory" life sentences for second serious offences

When do the courts impose these sentences?

There are two conditions which will have to apply.

The first is the "sentence condition":

• The person must be convicted of an offence which is

set out in Part 1 of new schedule 15B[146]
(which the *Explanatory Notes* refer to as "particularly serious sexual and violent offences")
• That offence must be serious enough to justify a sentence of imprisonment of 10 years or more.
The second is the "previous offence condition":
The person must previously have been convicted of an offence listed in any part of new schedule 15B[147]
• the person must have been sentenced to imprisonment for life or for a period of 10 years or more in respect of that previous offence
Does the court have discretion?

These provisions have been discussed as the latest version of a "two strikes and you're out" policy.

However, it is important to note that they do not require the courts to impose these sentences in all circumstances. The new section sets out that a "court must impose a life sentence" in the circumstances set out, unless it is of the opinion that there are particular circumstances that relate to the offence, or the previous offence or the offender, and which "would make it unjust to do so in all circumstances".

New extended sentences

The new rules

Section 125 of the *Legal Aid, Sentencing and Punishment of Offenders Act 2012* inserts two new sections into the 2003 Act which create new extended sentences for adults and juveniles. These can be imposed for the sexual and violent offences listed in Schedule 15 to the 2003 Act where certain conditions are met. For both sentences, the court must consider that the offender presents a substantial risk of causing serious harm through re-offending.

There are two further conditions for adults.
Either:
• the court must consider that the current offence is serious enough to merit a determinate sentence of at least four years;
Or
• at the time the present offence was committed the offender must have previously been convicted of an offence listed in new Schedule 15B.

The second of these alternative conditions does not apply to offenders aged under 18.

Where these conditions are made out, the court may impose an extended period for which the offender is to be subject to a licence (an 'extension period') of up to 5 years for a violent offence and up to 8 years for a sexual offence. Schedule 15 lists violent and sexual offences separately.

Sources and Notes

[1] House of Commons Library and
http://www.justice.gov.uk/statistics/prisons-and-probation/prison-population-figures

[2] Crime Punishment and the People: polling results – "It's Not You, It's them."

[3] Social Exclusion Unit. (2002). *Reducing re-offending by ex-prisoners.* London.

[4] Office of National Statistics and R Ford, *The Times*, 30 May 2011.

[5] "Number of offenders sent back to jail quadruples." *The Daily Telegraph*, 13 June 2011

[6] http://www.tynedaleheritage.org/Resources/GaolHist.htm

[7] http://www.vindolanda.com/

[8] John Podmore – "Out of Sight, Out of Mind" -2012 Biteback Books

[9] John Podmore – "Out of Sight, Out of Mind" -2012 Biteback Books

[10] John Podmore – "Out of Sight, Out of Mind" -2012 Biteback Books

[11] Hansard, House of Commons written answers, 14 November 2007

[12] http://www.cps.org.uk/publications/reports/inside-out-how-to-get-drugs-out-of-prison/

[13]
http://www.drugscope.org.uk/Resources/Drugscope/Documents/PDF/Good%20Practice/blakeyreport.pdf

[14] http://www.telegraph.co.uk/news/uknews/law-and-order/8976541/Prison-is-a-revolving-door-warns-watchdog.html

[15] http://www.telegraph.co.uk/news/uknews/law-and-order/8976541/Prison-is-a-revolving-door-warns-watchdog.html

[16] John Podmore – "Out of Sight, Out of Mind" -2012

Biteback Books
[17] John Podmore – "Out of Sight, Out of Mind" -2012
Biteback Books
[18]
http://www.hmprisonservice.gov.uk/assets/documents/100
03D1CHMPS_AR_main_2007-08.pdf
[19] http://www.official-
documents.gov.uk/document/hc0910/hc03/0323/0323.p
df
[20]
http://www.guardian.co.uk/society/2002/oct/04/publicvo
ices
[21]
http://www.justice.gov.uk/downloads/publications/hmipris
/2010/HMIP_AR_2008-9_web_published_rps.pdf
[22]
http://www.centreforsocialjustice.org.uk/default.asp?pageR
ef=341
[23]
http://www.centreforsocialjustice.org.uk/default.asp?pageR
ef=341
[24] Paul Burstow, parliamentary reply as Minister of State
Health 6/9/2012;
[25] http://www.centreforsocialjustice.org.uk
[26] Prison Reform Working Group. (2009). *Locked Up
Potential.* The Centre for Social Justice. London: The Centre
for Social Justice.
[27] *Community or Custody,* (2010) Make Justice Work
National Enquiry.
[28] Prison Reform Working Group. (2009). *Locked Up
Potential.* The Centre for Social Justice. London: The Centre
for Social Justice.
[29] National Audit Office, *Meeting Needs? The Offenders'
Learning and Skills Service*, London: The Stationary Office,
2008.
[30] http://olass.skillsfundingagency.bis.gov.uk/

[31] Prison Reform Working Group. (2009). *Locked Up Potential.* The Centre for Social Justice. London: The Centre for Social Justice.

[32] National Audit Office, *Meeting Needs? The Offenders' Learning and Skills Service*, London: The Stationary Office, 2008.

[33] Rule 32, *The Prison Rules 1999*. Rules consolidated Jan 2010.
http://www.hmprisonservice.gov.uk/assets/documents/100049 9Fprison_rules_1999_consolidated_jan_2010.pdf

[34] Ofsted *The Annual Report of Her Majesty's Chief Inspector of Education, Children's Services and Skills* 2009/10: page 94

[35] Prison Rules consolidated January 2010

[36] http://www.official-documents.gov.uk/document/hc1012/hc14/1454/1454.p df

[37] http://www.bis.gov.uk/assets/biscore/further-education-skills/docs/m/11-828-making-prisons-work-skills-for-rehabilitation

[38]
http://www.publications.parliament.uk/pa/cm200405/cms elect/cmeduski/114/11405.htm

[39]
http://www.publications.parliament.uk/pa/cm200405/cms elect/cmeduski/114/11405.htm

[40]
http://en.wikipedia.org/wiki/An_Officer_and_a_Gentleman

[41] http://www.shannontrust.org.uk/what-why.asp

[42] *The Prison Rules 1999*. Rules consolidated Jan 2010.
http://www.hmprisonservice.gov.uk/assets/documents/100049 9Fprison_rules_1999_consolidated_jan_2010.pdf

[43] Prison Reform Working Group. (2009). *Locked Up Potential.* The Centre for Social Justice. London: The Centre for Social Justice.

[44] Anne Widdecombe, 25th July 2011, interview with the Hexham Courant

[45] Reducing re-offending by ex-prisoners, http://www.socialexclusionunit.gov.uk/downloaddoc.asp?id=64

[46] Meredith Niles *"Breaking the cycle"*, The Charity Insight Essay, Issue 7 2011

[47] Meredith Niles *"Breaking the cycle"*, The Charity Insight Essay, Issue 7 2011

[48] Damian Hinds MP, 29th June 2011, House of Commons, Hansard, column 1049

[49] Centre for Social Justice *"Locked up Potential"*, March 2009

[50] Anna Soubry MP, 29th June 2011, House of Commons, Hansard, column 1034

[51] Blair Gibbs, 'If prisoners worked, we'd all be better off', The Telegraph, 12th June 2011

[52] http://www.parliament.uk/deposits/depositedpapers/2011/DEP2001-0759.zip

[53] Statistics.gov.uk, http://www.statistics.gov.uk/statbase/TSDdownload2.asp

[54] Home Affairs Committee, *Rehabilitation of Prisoners*, 7 January 2005, HC 193-I 2004-05: chapter 6

[55] ONE3ONE, Ministry of Justice, http://www.one3one.justice.gov.uk/a-fair-approach/code-of-practice/

[56] Huw Jenkins, Vice President DHL (Public Sector), http://www.one3one.justice.gov.uk/a-fair-approach/it-works-for-business/

[57] Paul, offender, HMP Wymott, http://www.one3one.justice.gov.uk/a-fair-approach/it-works-for-prisoners/

[58] Ken Clarke MP, Secretary of State for Justice, 29th June 2011, House of Commons, Hansard column 989

[59] Ken Clarke MP, Secretary of State for Justice, 29th June 2011, House of Commons, Hansard column 989

[60] David Burrows MP, 29th June 2011, House of Commons,

Hansard column 979

[61] David Burrows MP, 29th June 2011, House of Commons, Hansard column 979

[62] http://www.justice.gov.uk/downloads/consultations/green-paper-evidence-a.pdf#page=63

[63] http://www.justice.gov.uk/downloads/consultations/green-paper-evidence-a.pdf#page=63

[64] Meredith Niles *"Breaking the cycle"*, The Charity Insight Essay, Issue 7 2011

[65] Home Affairs Committee, *Rehabilitation of Prisoners*, 7 January 2005, HC 193-I 2004-05

[66] Damian Hinds MP, 29th June 2011, House of Commons, Hansard, column 1049

[67] Policy Exchange *"Inside Job"*, Blair Gibbs, 2011

[68] Policy Exchange *"Inside Job"*, Blair Gibbs, 2011

[69] Centre for Social Justice *"Locked up Potential"*, March 2009

[70] Meredith Niles *"Breaking the cycle"*, The Charity Insight Essay, Issue 7 2011

[71] Meredith Niles *"Breaking the cycle"*, The Charity Insight Essay, Issue 7 2011

[72] Meredith Niles *"Breaking the cycle"*, The Charity Insight Essay, Issue 7 2011

[73] Rob Owen, St. Giles Trust, Published in 'Justice Committee – Written Evidence *Cutting Crime: the case for justice reinvestment*,
http://www.publications.parliament.uk/pa/cm200910/cmselect/cmjust/94/94we61.htm

[74] http://www.blueskydevelopment.co.uk/

[75] http://www.blueskydevelopment.co.uk/

[76] http://www.blueskydevelopment.co.uk/

[77] http://research.dwp.gov.uk/asd/asd5/155summ.asp

[78]
http://www.telegraph.co.uk/comment/letters/8671717/We-need-high-speed-rail-because-more-people-use-trains-than-ever.html

[79] http://www.humshaughshop.co.uk/

[80] http://www.hexhamcommunity.net/

[81] http://www.hexhamcommunity.net/pages/number-28.php

[82] http://www.energyshare.com/hrh/

[83] Hexham Courant,
http://www.hexhamcourant.co.uk/news/news-at-a-glance/community-ambulance-plan-hatched-1.949081?referrerPath=1.930532

[84] http://www.betel.org.uk/

[85] http://www.theyworkforyou.com/debates/?id=2012-03-13a.132.1&s=speaker%3A24962#g132.2

[86] http://www.harrisfederation.org.uk/

[87] http://www.arkonline.org/

[88] Prison Reform Trust Report January 2005

[89]
http://www.publications.parliament.uk/pa/cm200405/cmselect/cmhaff/193/19315.htm

[90] http://www.smf.co.uk/media/news/prisons-minister-crispin-blunt-outlines-government-payment-by-re/

[91]
http://www.justice.gov.uk/news/features/feature131011a

[92] http://www.turning-point.co.uk/

[93] http://www.catch-22.org.uk

[94] The Reform Group, May 2011

[95]
http://www.justice.gov.uk/downloads/publications/hmipris/2011/hmip-annual-report-survey-summaries.pdf

[96]
http://www.justice.gov.uk/downloads/publications/corporate-reports/imb/annual-reports-2011/doncaster-2010-11.pdf

[97]
http://www.justice.gov.uk/downloads/publications/corporate-reports/imb/annual-reports-2011/doncaster-2010-11.pdf

[98]
http://www.publications.parliament.uk/pa/cm201011/cmhansrd/cm110503/text/110503w0001.htm#1105032400

0752

[99] http://www.insidetime.org/articleview.asp?a=242&c=not_all_bad_at_doncaster

[100] Home Office. *Community Safety Partnerships.* http://www.homeoffice.gov.uk/crime/partnerships (accessed August 2, 2011).

[101] Dedicated Drug Court Pilots A Process Report', *Matrix Knowledge Group* (for Ministry of Justice), April 2008: http://www.matrixknowledge.co.uk/wp-content/uploads/dedicated-drug-courts2.pdf

[102] Kerr, J. et al., 'The Dedicated Drug Courts Pilot Evaluation Process Study', *Ministry of Justice*, January 2011, p. i: http://www.justice.gov.uk/publications/docs/ddc-process-evaluation-study.pdf

[103] http://www.centreforsocialjustice.org.uk/default.asp?pageRef=341

[104] Ford, Richard. "Criminals who reoffend are less likely to be jailed again." *The Times*, 30 May 2011.

[105] Daily Telegraph. "Number of offenders sent back to jail quadruples." *The Daily Telegraph*, 13 June 2011: 2.

[106] National Audit Office, *Offenders on Short Custodial Sentences Summary*, p7

[107] Bromley Trust, *Bromley Briefings Prison Factfile* June 2011 p7

[108] Bromley Trust, *Bromley Briefings Prison Factfile* June 2011 p7.

[109] Home Office, *Justice For All*, CM 5563, July 2002, p12

[110] HL Deb, 4 May 2006, c566

[111] HL Deb, 18 October 2006, c185W

[112] HL Deb, 4 May 2006, c566

[113] National Audit Office, *Managing Offenders on Short Custodial Sentences Summary*, p2

[114] Verkaik, R. (2009, September 17). *Cash crisis in prisoner rehabilitation scheme adds to overcrowding.* Retrieved July

31, 2011, from The Independent on Sunday:
http://www.independent.co.uk/news/uk/crime/cash-crisis-in-prisoner-rehabilitation-scheme-adds-to-overcrowding-1788700.html

[115] Lord Carlile is a Liberal Democrat Member of the House of Lords. Lord Carlile has previously worked closely with the Howard League for Penal Reform

[116] Criminal Justice Joint Inspection. (2010). *Indeterminate Sentences for Public Protection: A Joint Inspection by HMI Probation and HMI Prisons*. Criminal Justice Joint Inspectorate. London: Criminal Justice Joint Inspection.

[117] Jacobson, J., & Hough, M. (2010). *Unjust Deserts: Imprisonment for Public Protection*. Prison Reform Trust. London: Prison Reform Trust.

[118] Jacobson, J., & Hough, M. (2010). *Unjust Deserts: Imprisonment for Public Protection*. Prison Reform Trust. London: Prison Reform Trust.

[119] Prison Reform Trust. (2010). *Indefinitely Maybe? How the indeterminate sentence for public protection is unjust and unsustainable.*

[120] Hansard HC, 26 January 2010, c732W

[121] Table A3.4, Ministry of Justice (2011) Offender Management Caseload Statistics 2010, London: Ministry of Justice

[122] HM Chief Inspector of Prisons, HM Chief Inspector of Probation (2008) The indeterminate sentence for public protection: A thematic review, London: HM Prisons Inspectorate

[123]
http://www.publications.parliament.uk/pa/cm201011/cmhansrd/cm111101/debtext/111101-0002.htm#11110189000735

[124] Crook, F. (2011, June 29). *Penal Reform: Where is Labour?* Retrieved August 3, 2011, from Howard League for Penal Reform:
http://www.howardleague.org/francescrookblog/penal-

reform-where-is-labour

[125] Secretary of State for Justice v James and Lee [2009] UKHL 22 (House of Lords May 6, 2009)

[126] Secretary of State for Justice v James and Lee [2009] UKHL 22 (House of Lords May 6, 2009)

[127] Secretary of State for Justice v James and Lee [2009] UKHL 22 (House of Lords May 6, 2009)

[128] A fuller transcript of the House of Lords' destruction of this policy is set out in Appendix 3 at the end of this book, along with the old and new statutory sections at appendix 4-5.

[129] Ministry of Justice. (2010, December). Breaking the Cycle: Effective Punishment, Rehabilitation and Sentencing of Offenders. London: Ministry of Justice.

[130] Ministry of Justice. (2010, December). Breaking the Cycle: Effective Punishment, Rehabilitation and Sentencing of Offenders. London: Ministry of Justice.

[131] Sunday Times, Dominic Lawson, June 17 2012

[132]

http://sentencingcouncil.judiciary.gov.uk/sentencing/indeterminate-prison-sentences.htm

[133] For those aged under 18 these sentences are termed Custody for Life and Detention for Public Protection respectively.

[134] However after ten years of this licence, the offender can apply to the Parole Board for it to be cancelled. If they are unsuccessful they can then try again each year to have it reconsidered.

[135] 225 Life sentence or imprisonment for public protection for serious offences

(1)   This section applies where— (a) a person aged 18 or over is convicted of a serious offence committed after the commencement of this section, and (b) the court is of the opinion that there is a significant risk to members of the public of serious harm occasioned by the commission by him of further specified offences.

(2) If— (a) the offence is one in respect of which the offender

would apart from this

section be liable to imprisonment for life, and (b) the court considers that the seriousness of the offence, or of the offence and one or more offences associated with it, is such as to justify the imposition of a sentence of imprisonment for life, the court must impose a sentence of imprisonment for life.

(3) In a case not falling within subsection (2), the court must impose a sentence of imprisonment for public protection.

(4) A sentence of imprisonment for public protection is a sentence of imprisonment for an indeterminate period, subject to the provisions of Chapter 2 of Part 2 of the Crime (Sentences) Act 1997 (c. 43) as to the release of prisoners and duration of licenses.

(5) An offence the sentence for which is imposed under this section is not to be regarded as an offence the sentence for which is fixed by law.

[136] Categories of which are set out in schedule 15 of the Criminal Justice Act 2003

[137] 13 Sentences of imprisonment for public protection

(1) In section 225 of the Criminal Justice Act 2003 (life sentence or imprisonment for public protection), for subsection (3) substitute:

(3) In a case not falling within subsection (2), the court may impose a sentence of imprisonment for public protection if the condition in subsection (3A) or the condition in subsection (3B) is met.

(3A) The condition in this subsection is that, at the time the offence was committed, the offender had been convicted of an offence specified in Schedule 15A.

(3B) The Condition in this subsection is that the notional minimum term is at least two years.

(3C) The notional minimum term is part of the sentence that the court would specify under section 82A(2) of the Sentencing Act (determination of tariff) if it imposed a sentence of imprisonment for public protection but was required to disregard the matter mentioned in section

82A(3)(b) of that Act (crediting periods of remand).
(2) After Schedule 15 to that Act, insert the Schedule set out in Schedule 5 to this Act.

[138] A list of qualifying offences being mentioned in schedule 15A of the 2008 Act.

[139] Article 5 (4): "Everyone who is deprived of his liberty by arrest or detention shall be entitled to take proceedings by which the lawfulness of his detention shall be decided speedily by a court and his release ordered if the detention is not lawful. "

[140] Article 5 (1) (a-f): "Everyone has the right to liberty and security of person/ No one shall be deprived of his liberty save in the following cases and in accordance with a procedure prescribed by law. "

[141] Secretary of State for Justice (Respondent) v James (FC) (Appellant) (formerly Walker and another) R (on the application of Lee) (FC) (Appellant) v Secretary of State for Justice (Respondent) and one other action, [2009] UKHL 22 (House of Lords May 6, 2009)

[142] Ibid

[143] Secretary of State for Justice (Respondent) v James (FC) (Appellant) (formerly Walker and another) R (on the application of Lee) (FC) (Appellant) v Secretary of State for Justice (Respondent) and one other action, [2009] UKHL 22 (House of Lords May 6, 2009)

[144] With thanks to Pat Strickland of the Home Affairs Section of the House of Commons Library, who helped prepare this short summary of the changed provisions

[145] Subsection (1) of new section 224A to the *Criminal Justice Act 2003*, as inserted by section 122 of the *Legal Aid, Sentencing and Punishment of Offenders Act 2012*

[146] inserted by schedule 18 of the 2012 Act

[147] This adds equivalent offences committed under service law or in other jurisdictions, as well as murder to the list of serious violent and sexual offences

INDEX